AIRFIX
magazine
annual
for modellers
1973

edited by Chris Ellis

PSL Patrick Stephens, London
in association with
AIRFIX Airfix Products Ltd

First published—September 1972.

ISBN 0 85059 095 7.

Text set in 9 on 10 pt Times Roman. Printed in Great Britain on Fineblade Brochure 100 gm² for Patrick Stephens Limited, 9 Ely Place, London EC1N 6SQ, by Blackfriars Press Limited, Leicester LE5 4BS. Bound by Hunter & Foulis Limited, Edinburgh EH7 4NP.

Editor's introduction

THIS IS THE SECOND *Airfix Magazine Annual for Modellers,* following closely the style and format of the first issue last year which met with huge approval from plastic modelling enthusiasts. So great was the demand, in fact, that we had to reprint within a couple of weeks of publication. Once again, this time we have aimed to bring you a selection of articles by leading *Airfix Magazine* contributors, in many cases taking advantage of the more generous space offered in book form to provide articles longer than could possibly be carried in *Airfix Magazine.*

Readers of both *Airfix Magazine Annual* and *Airfix Magazine* come with all degrees of skill and experience. Some of you reading this might never have tried making a plastic construction kit; others may have been making them for nearly 20 years. We've included some fairly simple models here for the absolute beginner; those who like the Airfix 00/HO size model soldier figures will find the 'Armies by the Dozen' article useful, for instance. You need little more than a set of model paints to start creating new model soldiers from the Airfix miniatures. Similarly, aircraft enthusiasts can make some simple but original looking models by repainting existing kits to depict the Irish Air Corps machines illustrated and drawn here. For the more experienced modeller there is an Avro Manchester conversion (revised and repeated from *Airfix Magazine* by popular request), and a lengthy article by Gerald Scarborough which gives expert tips for modelling military vehicles from scratch. Older readers can join former IPMS President Fred Henderson for a look back to pre-war modelling, and youngsters can see what they missed! Our popular 'Photopage' feature from *Airfix Magazine* gets a jumbo-size section here in the Annual. All these and many more features for your enjoyment appear in these pages. One of our functions is to generate a few new ideas and we hope you'll possibly find a few more modelling interests in the pages which follow.

We would like to thank all contributors to this edition, and finally we thank you, the reader, for your continuing enthusiasm and interest in the fascinating world of plastic kit modelling.

CHRIS ELLIS.

Contents

Cover illustrations. Main picture: *BAC Jaguar in RAF markings as modelled by Airfix.* **Bottom, left to right:** *Diorama by Roy Dilley based on a standard plastic kit with much modified Britain's figures. An LGB narrow gauge train on Bert Lamkin's outdoor railway. Irish Air Corps T9 Spitfire conversion by Chris Ellis.*

Back cover: *Napoleonic troops in a brisk tabletop engagement. Numerous conversions of Airfix 00/HO figures can be made using the simple techniques described in* Armies by the Dozen *(Photo courtesy Croydon Advertiser). World War 1 lorry belonging to the Royal Navy. The model is scratch-built. A Royal Navy Sea King demonstrates its versatility.*

AN EYE FOR DETAIL

By Bryan Philpott

Above: *This superb model shows the effect skill and patience can achieve. The basic model is Airfix's* Royal Sovereign, *with the complete rigging and ratlines built from scratch. No job for fumbling fingers, this.*

Right: *Another Airfix kit, the Focke-Wulf 189A-2, displayed in a cold-looking Russian front diorama by Newcastle modeller T. J. Quinn. Note the character given to this model by the figures and open cockpit canopy, and the attention to detail shown in the snowy footprints on the wings.*

Below left: *One of the recently-introduced vacuum-formed models, a German A7V from World War 1, with scratch-built machine guns. Careful painting lifts this model above the average.* **Below right:** *Super-detailed Airfix 1:32 scale Ford Capri in Rally setting by Denis Johnstone of Belfast. Features include slot-car wheels filed to look like Minilites, vinyl roof from masking tape painted semi-matt black, bonnet scoop from plastic card and mud screen from clear plastic card.*

HOWEVER WELL ASSEMBLED and carefully painted a model may be there is often an undefinable 'something' missing that prevents it from capturing the true atmosphere of the original. Aircraft, like people, have character and it is often this hard-to-define element that is missing. If one studies photographs or actual aircraft in their normal environments, it soon becomes apparent that each has its own personality, which if captured in miniature can make a world of difference between a good model and an excellent one. The seemingly nose-heavy pose of Meteors, the sinister squat of the Harrier, the graceful lines of the Hunter and the pugnacious air of a fully armed Phantom, are just a few illustrations to show the general theme of character and atmosphere that can be captured to advantage.

Quite often just the addition of a few extra details and the tidying up of some of the kit components can go a long way to achieving an air of

realism, and the purpose of this short article is to outline some of the basic materials and approaches that can be gainfully used by the keen modeller.

One of the most simple operations that nearly always enhances the appearance of a model is the opening of the canopy, but if this is done it is necessary to carry out some detail work to the interior of the cockpit. On most of the larger scale models manufacturers include a certain amount of detail but on smaller scales, due to considerations of cost, etc, this is not always possible. In any form of detailing the main essential is to obtain good basic research material and this is not too hard to come by if the modeller is determined enough. On such a small scale as 1:72 it is not really essential to ensure that every instrument, lever and push-button is faithfully reproduced; in fact it is not too difficult to arrive at a basic instrument panel that will be sufficient for most 1939-45 fighters. It

Above left: *IFF aerials being fitted to a 1:48 scale Spitfire Vb by the UHU glue and cocktail stick method described in the text.* **Above right:** *A. G. Bell's PzKpfw III Ausf J/L conversion based on the Airfix Stug III and PzKpfw IV kits with additional components fabricated from plastic card. Note the effective use of dry-brushed paint to simulate a weathered appearance.*

is of interest to note, however, that some of the specialist decal makers, notably Modeldecal, now include tiny decals for instrument panels of specific aircraft on their sheets of transfers.

Where the luxury of a printed panel is not available, however, you need to make your own. Once the layout has been decided upon the panel can be made from two sheets of thin plastic card or even cardboard. Paint one gloss black and the other matt black or grey, then with a small drill make holes in the matt panel and when satisfied that these are correct cement the two together. The gloss black will now shine through the holes, thus simulating glass. The addition of red and yellow spots and lines can represent switches, fire warning lights and other instruments. Once this one assembly is mounted in the fuselage the difference it makes to the completed model will begin to be seen. Naturally a seat should be provided and this can either be made from scrap or can be the one supplied with the kit, reworked to the correct appearance.

Right: *Some kits contain excellent detail in their out-of-the-box form, and the Airfix 1:12 scale 4½-litre supercharged Bentley is certainly one. The 272 parts in this kit include rubber-tyred wheels, plated radiator, and opening bonnet showing a nicely detailed engine.*

In many early offerings from the manufacturers, seats are often just a 'L'-shaped piece of plastic, but it is surprising just what can be achieved by the addition of shaped plastic card sides and straps. The latter can be made from Sellotape painted the correct colour, drafting tape (which has a texture similar to the webbing material used on safety harnesses), or even odd material 'borrowed' from the lady of the house. Buckles and fasteners reproduced from stretched sprue and painted silver add an authentic touch to this piece of vital equipment. A good source of seats, incidentally, are the Airfix 1:76 scale vehicle kits which in some cases have neat bucket seats. If the canopy is to be opened, one strap of the safety harness can be left hanging over the side of the cockpit coaming, and this small addition will be worth more than its weight in gold in adding to the character of the completed model. Control columns and rudder pedals, as

Above: *The Airfix 1:76 scale T34/85 is a very simple model, but a little thought can make it into something really worthwhile. A dozer blade has been added to this version, the commander's hatch cut open, and the tracks made to sag by inserting small pieces of scrap plastic under the running boards (C. O. Ellis).*

Above: *Model Focke-Wulf 190 weathered by the rub-and-buff method mentioned in the text.*

Above: *The various aerials which appeared on Meteor 8 aircraft are reproduced on this Frog model with toothbrush bristles and stretched sprue.* **Right:** *One of a number of Airfix Lightnings constructed and detailed by Northampton modeller C. A. Griggs. The markings on this, and the two Lightnings below, have all been painted on by hand!*

well as flap, throttle and undercarriage retraction levers can all be fabricated from sprue or items in the spares box and help to give a furnished look to the pilot's 'office'.

There are, of course, many other ways to make instrument panels and other equipment, and one of the joys of modelling is discovering such things for oneself.

Turning to the exterior of the model, replacement of the over-thick undercarriage doors by plastic card ones is not difficult and always pays dividends. Use the originals as patterns to draw new ones on plastic card. Similarly, attention to other parts of the airframe will also bring their reward. Pitot tubes, aerials and guns can be reworked to give a more accurate scale appearance, and it is in such fine detail as this that the aircraft's character can be captured. Quite often the main aerial post of a 1939-45 bomber or fighter looks more suitable for carrying a 33 kv power line than a fine wire aerial, but attention with 'wet and dry' paper will soon reduce the thickness to an acceptable standard. Aerials themselves are often shown by the use of nylon thread or, worse still, cotton; by far the best method is the use of stretched sprue which is easily attached to the aerial post and fin, and just as easily replaced should it become broken at a later date. The best sprue to use for this is the clear variety that surrounds the canopies, or alternatively grey or silver sprue that comes in some kits.

Another good substitute, albeit harder to apply until the secret is learned, is UHU glue. This rubber-based impact adhesive will stretch to incredible lengths and, if applied correctly, can often look better than sprue. The best method to use is to squeeze some UHU on to a clean piece of paper, take a well-pointed cocktail stick, dip it into the UHU, twist it so that the glue adheres then gently apply the pointed stick to the aerial post

and slowly pull it along to where the other end of the aerial is to be attached. As UHU tends to 'go off' quite quickly it is usually necessary to squeeze a fresh supply for every aerial needed on a model, but this is no hardship and as only a little is used at a time expense is negligible. First attempts will probably result in an aerial of varying thicknesses or failure to stretch the UHU to its attachment point but, as with everything connected with modelling, practice makes perfect. This method, once mastered, can be used to rig biplanes and has the advantage that it is even easier to replace than sprue; but one disadvantage is that it is so fine that it is hard to see, which makes it very vulnerable if a model is handled frequently.

Whilst on the subject of aerials, it is worth considering the addition of the various whip aerials, navigational aid aerials and electronic equipment antennae that adorn modern aircraft. In most kits of modern jet aircraft such parts are more often than not omitted simply because there is no easy way of including them in the kit. Such omissions can easily be rectified by the use of that frequently mentioned commodity, stretched sprue. Personal observation of aircraft at air displays and study of photographs will soon reveal the positions of the many aerials that exist; sprue can be used to simulate all these and by careful manipulation of it various thicknesses can be obtained.

Attachment of such aerials may at first seem to be difficult, but the use

Above: The Airfix HMS Prince *model in its from-the-box form. Compare this with the* Royal Sovereign *on page four.*

of a dentist's or watch maker's fine burr will soon produce a hole into which the sprue can be fitted. If the acquisition of a watch maker's drill is beyond the pocket, or the dentist is not friendly enough to approach, then a hot pin can be used, but extreme care is needed—unless this method is used carefully the required hole can soon look like battle damage! Fuel vents, flap jacks and steps can be made in similar ways but discretion must be used as it is easy to overdo it and end up with a Christmas tree effect. Fuse wire is also a useful commodity to keep handy as this can make hydraulic lines and aerials as well as the other odd part for which sprue or plastic rod may not be suited.

Most aircraft, when at rest, have their control surfaces, such as ailerons, elevators, rudders and flaps, in various positions, and once again study of photographs will soon reveal the characteristic positions of such components. If going to this length is of interest then remember that ailerons work in opposition to each other, and other surfaces do not usually have too pronounced a movement about their normal axis. Shortening of undercarriage legs plus the addition of brake pipes and retraction jacks are other areas where the super detailer can come into his own, but once again the watchword is discretion. One useful modification that can be made is the flattening of the bottom of wheels simulating the weight of the aircraft. This particularly pays dividends when a heavy bomber is concerned, as nothing looks more faked than a model Lancaster perched on two perfectly round tyres.

Finally, attention to navigation and landing lights is always worth while, so instead of making do by painting these, look out for red, green and other coloured plastic cocktail sticks which can easily be cut up and shaped. Reflectors for landing lights can be simply simulated with cooking foil or silver paper which can also be used for grills in air intakes, especially if it is obtained from cigarette packets when it will have a texture not unlike wire mesh.

It would be possible to go on at great length but one of the joys of modelling is finding out for oneself, so with the few ideas given it is hoped that the seeds will have been planted for the average modeller to start looking for ways and means of turning an eye to detail. Some pictures here show what can be achieved. Time spent in trying to capture an aircraft's character is more rewarding than attempting to add working undercarriages, removable cowlings and other such gimmicks that are really for toys and not serious models. What it boils down to in the long run is the need for reference, research, and observation. Ideas for added detailing come most easily from a study of pictures in books. A model made straight from the kit will probably have closed canopy, and rigid controls. If you see a picture of a Spitfire in a dispersal bay it will probably have its canopy open and drooping control surfaces. Try working such effects into a model and you'll see how quickly your model will take on a character of its own.

Below: Dornier Do 217K with aerials from sprue and UHU.

BASIC MILITARY VEHICLE MODELLING

By Gerald Scarborough

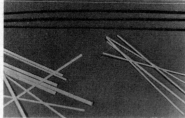

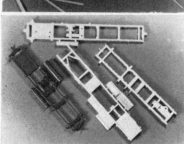

Above, top to bottom: *Basic tools: To the rear is a razor saw, then, in order, a six-inch ruler wrapped with 'Wet and Dry' paper, three spring hair clips and a hat pin, compass, tweezers, three craft knives, nail scissors, pin chuck, small drills and triangular section file. The only other thing needed is a steel rule. Plastic card of 60, 40, 30, 20 and 10 thou thicknesses. Plastic rod to the rear, Microstrip to the left and Superfine strip to the right. Some Airfix chassis; at rear, AEC Refueling Tanker; left to right, Matador 5.5 inch Gun Tractor, Austin Fire Tender, Bedford Refueler.*

MANY MODELLERS must have admired scratch-built replicas of trucks or armoured cars, but not so many will have attempted to make such models for themselves. In the popular 1:76 scale of Airfix AFV kits, scratch-building is an excellent way of expanding a collection. As far as trucks and armoured cars go, the work is not too difficult. Railway modellers seeking to make roadside commercial vehicles should also find the methods of building useful to know.

Tools

It's amazing how few tools you really need to work in plastic, in fact no more than you would normally use on a plastic kit. Most people will already have a craft knife, maybe even one of the expensive sets with many different blades, but there's only one blade that I consider essential and that's the usual curved one. Two others that I use fairly regularly are the straight and the hooked, though these are less essential. A steel ruler is a must, to ensure good straight cuts and scoring as well as for measuring and marking out parts. A good solid pair of compasses is the third essential to use for marking out, of course, but also for scoring in planking, impressing rivet detail, and enlarging holes. There are all sorts of jobs where the point will come in handy. If you have an old dart it will serve for a lot of these jobs, and the point can always be sharpened on an oilstone. A few bits of fine sandpaper or 'wet and dry' paper complete the basic outfit.

There are still a few tools that can be used (to make life easier) which you can acquire as funds are available. You may even have them about the house already. There will come a time when you have to saw some of the thicker plastic sheet or remove unwanted parts from a kit and here the razor saw is ideal and is available for about £1, give or take the odd pence, but if you can't run to that most households boast a Junior 6 inch hacksaw, and in fact I used one of these for years. Drills again should be about most homes but you may have to buy a few of the very small sizes like a $\frac{1}{32}$ or $\frac{1}{16}$ inch. A small pin-chuck to hold the smallest is also useful but I manage to use the larger sizes by twirling between finger and thumb as plastic is so easy to drill. The way I work it is to have a nice fine drill in the pin chuck for drilling pilot holes which are then opened out by the appropriate larger size. A piece of piano wire with the end clipped off at an angle makes a makeshift drill for opening out holes, as does the tang of a small file. A simple pin, held in a pair of pliers and heated in a candle flame, can be used for 'drilling' or even making slots, but do practice on scrap first as it's only by experience that you'll learn to judge the right heat. If you can borrow a leather punch they are useful for making plastic discs to use as hub or radiator caps and mirrors, etc, but they are not enough use to warrant the expenditure as they cause too much distortion in the surrounding plastic if used for punching holes in parts.

Files I find of limited use, it's often easier to carve material away with the knife or use sandpaper wrapped round a 6 inch wooden ruler (probably my favourite 'tool' this); in fact the only file I use regularly is of triangular section, fine cut, about $5\frac{1}{2}$ inches long, and is handy for getting into corners. Manicure scissors and nail clippers are also useful household tools that you can adapt. Even a nail file will sometimes come in handy,

Above: *German medium truck, the Krupp L3H 163, scale plans of which appear below. This is a fairly easy model to build but really needs side racks adding to make it authentic.*

and of course, a pair of tweezers. Don't make yourself unpopular by chopping about on the best table. Make a work surface from a sheet of hardboard about 1 foot × 1 foot 6 inches, and keep a bit of cardboard to rest your tube of cement on before it drips all over the place. I say hardboard because it's better than a wooden board and, of course, there's no grain to set your knife wandering off at an angle when you're trying to cut straight. Hardboard is cheap, and you should be able to beg an offcut from somewhere. Sellotape (or similar brands of adhesive tape) can also be classed as a 'tool'. It's ideal for holding parts together while they dry though occasionally elastic bands can be used. Useful again for these holding jobs are cheap hair clips from chain stores. These are made from aluminium and are spring loaded with a nice gentle grip. Get into the

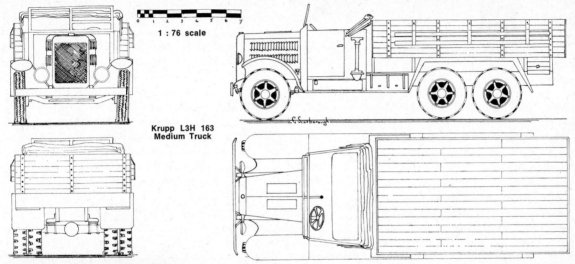

1 : 76 scale

Krupp L3H 163
Medium Truck

habit of collecting bits and bobs like these, or even buying them when you have a few pence to spare. This goes for almost anything made from plastic like old ball pens, broken toys, cocktail sticks—all sorts of things want adding to a bits box.

Materials

Most military vehicle models will be based on some plastic kit and here the Airfix range alone provides many options for simple conversions or parts from these can be incorporated in more ambitious projects. These kits are your raw material so never throw unused parts away, store them in a spares box, or file them away in the original box or packet so that they are easily available. The Minitank range of ready-made models (to the smaller 1:87 scale) can also provide useful parts if models from the range are 'cannibalised'.

For main construction work sheet plastic, usually referred to as plastic or styrene card, is used and this comes in various sizes of sheet in thicknesses of .005, .010, .015, .020, .030, .040 and .060 inch. These are commonly referred to as 5 thou (ie 5 thousandths of an inch), 10 thou, etc, and the most useful for vehicles are 10 thou, 20 thou and possibly 30 thou. The larger thicknesses are handy to have available but I have made many models using only the 10 and 20 thou card. These have a decided advantage in that they are easy to cut and work, are cheap, and can of course be laminated (ie sandwiched together) to any thickness you require. Brand names for this material include Plastikard, Rikokard and Polycard, plus many more.

You may already have read construction articles in *Airfix Magazine* referring to Microstrip, which is just about the most useful stuff to have in your raw materials store. It is, in fact, thin slivers of plastic strip, 3 inches long, cut cleanly and without curl from various thicknesses of

Above: *A few little extras like an open door, driving mirror, additional fuel and water cans, camouflage nets, armament and crew help the final effect on these two models of a Bedford Troop Carrier and a modified Jeep from the Buffalo kit detailed up as a Long Range Desert Group vehicle.*

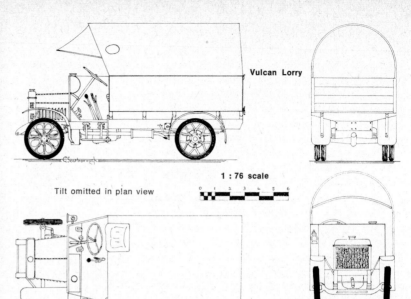

Vulcan Lorry

Tilt omitted in plan view

1 : 76 scale

Above top: *Vulcan lorry shown in component parts. A scale plan for this model appears at right.* **Above bottom:** *Completed model of the Vulcan lorry impressed into Army service during 1914-18. Small dioramas like this can easily be built up with little more than sand or other material that gives a realistic base, and a few well-selected figures, perhaps with some small alterations to their basic positions.*

Above top: *An early Gerald Scarborough model of a Chevrolet C8A, built using wheels from a DUKW and plastic card.* **Above bottom:** *Morris CD/SW 6 × 4 breakdown truck using DUKW wheels. This again is an early Gerald Scarborough model which used the nearest wheels available at the time. With the much larger range of wheels on the market now it is easier to find more suitable items than the ones used.*

plastic card. It again comes in various widths and thicknesses but for our purpose the one to go for is a packet of assorted which contains one gross of strips for about 25p. Also available is a Superfine Microstrip which is invaluable if you have a special job like a crane jib or the Queen Mary Semi-trailer illustrated in this article on page 12.

The final type of plastic available is in rod form, in lengths of up to 12 inches and in sizes of 30 thou, 40 thou and 50 thou diameter or again as an assorted pack of 24 for about 15p. Shorter rods of this type are sold in the Mopok range.

Just to re-cap, all you need to make a start with is a sheet each of 10, 20 and 30 thou plastic card, a packet of assorted Microstrip and one of assorted rod.

Working in plastic

As you will know plastic will stand a lot of abuse, but two things it doesn't like are excessive heat and great blobs of adhesive. Bear in mind that friction means heat; therefore, when sawing, filing or sandpapering take it easy and with a gentle touch. In fact for sanding, when convenient, it is best to use 'wet and dry' paper. Used wet it cuts remarkably well and the plastic stays cool. For final sanding on a partly built model it can, of course, be used dry, and a good tip is to wrap a small piece round a wooden six-inch ruler or similar size piece of wood (rather than use it loose in the hand) as this makes it easier to preserve a straight edge where necessary. For cutting plastic card, use a steel rule and a sharp craft knife, but again don't use too much force otherwise the edge of the plastic will distort. Keep your fingers well out of the path of the blade, in fact treat your knife with respect, keep a firm grip on the handle and *never* force it, as it may slip or break the blade, and then the blood will flow. Yours! To come back to cutting, the thicker sheets can be cut part through and then snapped off cleanly.

We have mentioned plastic's aversion to heat but this can be used to advantage if controlled, to mould, bend, stretch or even make holes in it. The most common moulding job on vehicles is mudguards and these are really simple to do. First study the style; if they are 'rounded' edged you will need to allow sufficient thickness of material to be able to sand them to the correct section. Cut a strip the width of the mudguard and of sufficient length and thickness, wrap this round a nice smooth wooden dowel of the correct diameter and bind in place, not too tight, with soft wool to hold in shape. Now place this in a basin (or a teacup will do) and pour

Above top: *Steyr 640 Heavy Car; note the use of figures taken from other kits to depict a captured pilot being taken to a POW 'cage'.* **Above bottom:** *Another type of German car, this one an Auto Union/Horch using Land Rover wheels with the rest scratch built; again the figures are suitably converted ones from other kits (Top model by Mike Bell).*

Above top: *Volkswagen with wheels from a Matchbox toy. Built from a Bellona print, the body detail was cut from 10 thou plastic card, although this could have been done from stretched sprue if desired.* **Above bottom:** *Bellona Prints provided the plans for this Hanomag Troop Carrier built for wargaming. The roadwheels are cut down from those supplied with the 88 mm Flak Gun Tractor, the simple tracks are laminations of strip cut from 10 thou plastic card.*

boiling water in to cover well. Leave for at least 30 seconds or so (the time will depend on the thickness of the plastic, but you'll learn with experience), then remove and hold in cold water to set the shape. Simply remove the wool binding and then slide the mudguards off the dowel ready for trimming to final length and shaping the edges and ends as necessary.

There is enough heat in a candle flame to heat up a pin, held in small pliers, or a compass point, which can then be used to 'drill' holes in card, etc, or even cut slots or weld parts together. The point to watch is to get the heat right; practice on scraps of card will soon give you experience and confidence before trying it on a model. Rod and Microstrip can also be bent round the compasses to an acute curve for such things as vehicle tilt frames, but here the heat required is not so great. Again practice is the thing, and you will soon find all sorts of applications for this technique.

While we have the candle available there's the knack of stretching sprue which is most frustrating until you learn to do it. The technique is quickly described but considerable practice is needed to perfect it.

First take a length of sprue from any plastic kit, hold it about an inch above a steady candle flame until it starts to go 'floppy' and with a wet look on the surface. Then withdraw well away from the flame and gently pull the ends apart until the molten portion stretches. You can, by this method, pull various thicknesses right down to cobweb size but do give time for it to set after stretching, otherwise it will curl up if released too early. Your first few will probably snap through snatching too quickly but after plenty of practice you'll be able to pull any thickness you want.

There's just one other use of the candle flame that comes to mind and that's for making 'nails' as we'll call them. Once you can heat-stretch sprue cut off a short length, not too thin, and hold the end to the side of the flame and watch the plastic melt and roll back to form a head. These little nails are ideal for gear levers or working hinge pins and larger ones can be cut off and used for sidelights.

Finally there's the stuff for sticking the bits together, of which the most familiar will be tube polystyrene cement. Very useful, but it does have a tendency to string a bit. A wooden cocktail stick is ideal for applying it to the model or even a sharpened match or hat pin will do. Always stand the tube on a piece of cardboard, then if it does drip it won't do any harm. The snag is that plastic card doesn't seem to stick too well with tube cement and you'll find that a bottle of liquid glue, like Mek-Pak, will give better results. This is applied with a nice pointed brush; the pieces to be joined are held in place and it is just brushed sparingly into the join. If too much should run in just blow it off quickly but watch your direction. It evaporates very quickly so get the top on the bottle immediately after use. A combination of the two adhesives is often very useful—tack parts in place with the minimum of tube cement and then complete the join with liquid cement.

Of limited use on vehicle models is Body Putty or Plastic Padding which can be used for filling unwanted cracks, but there shouldn't be a lot of need for it if you take care with the building in the first place. There is just one odd use for Plastic Padding but I'll come to that when we build a vehicle in detail.

Model choice

We've discussed tools and materials and a little bit of technique and now come to the actual vehicle we want to model. I shall have to presume that you've made up a fair number of Airfix kits and now want to try your hand on some modifications and simple scratch-builds. If you are a war-games enthusiast you'll probably not require such a high standard of detail finish; in fact this would be inadvisable as constant handling will soon remove things like driving mirrors, etc, and I'd also suggest that bodies of trucks be made of thicker plastic and the attachment of axles be strengthened. In fact, aim at rigidity rather than scale frailty.

Above top: *When you have a bit more experience you can try this Queen Mary aircraft trailer with Bedford tractor unit. The entire trailer is scratch built; full details of this model appear in the February 1972 issue of Airfix Magazine.* Above bottom: *Austin K6/ZB Signals/Wireless Van based on the Fire Tender chassis with a scratch built body.*

Above top: *Highly detailed Long Range Desert Group Chevrolet. Note the informal crew and extra cans and equipment packed aboard.* Above bottom: *Another variation on the Steyr 640 Heavy Car, this time the Ambulance version with the Afrika Korps 'Palm and Swastika' emblem painted on the half-open door. (Both models by Mick Bell).*

If your aim is a representative collection of showpiece military vehicles then you will obviously want to include as much detail as possible, and this I will deal with later. If you want a vehicle as 'background' in a diorama something between the first two styles will probably be required, not too simple but unobtrusive so that it doesn't detract the eye from the main theme of the display.

Actually the 'glass case' model will often look better if set on a small base of representative terrain. This sort of model must be planned before it's even started as a lot can be built in to make it look natural. For example, it's no good building it four-square on a flat surface if it will be displayed traversing rough ground. Get the axles set by bending or flattening the springs and building in a 'lean' to one side and turning the steering a bit as well to help the effect. Effect is what we're after, as a model that is maybe not 100 per cent accurate can often depict the character of a vehicle better than the most accurate of models. To this end do study photographs of all vehicles, as many as you can get hold of, watch them in films, on television, study the way they behave on the road, braking, turning, up hill down dale, and you'll gradually be able to understand their characteristics and behaviour.

Above all keep your eye open for old military trucks still in use. They are still to be found round the backs of garages, probably converted to breakdown trucks, on fairgrounds, farms, timber yards, forestry and contractors' sites, pits and quarries. If possible keep a camera handy, and a tape and sketch pad, as these are the best opportunities you'll get of obtaining those little extra details. However there may be modifications that have been made on some of these ex-service vehicles which are not too obvious at first glance yet which have nothing to do with the vehicle's original appearance.

Unless you are fortunate to drop on a 'mint' condition vehicle and are capable of doing your own scale drawings, you will need to buy the plans from which to work. Fortunately there is a large range of these available in 1:76 (ie 4 mm : 1 foot) scale, all at reasonable prices. I suggest you write, sending a stamped, addressed envelope, for the list of drawings currently available. John B. Church, 'Honeywood', Middle Road, Tiptoe, Nr Lymington, Hampshire, has mostly British, American and Canadian vehicles covered in his extensive range while Len Morgan, 45 Goldsworthy Gardens, Silwood Street, London SE16 2TB, has a long list of drawings, mostly German and Italian vehicles drawn up by M. Bell. All these give at least four views of the subject vehicle and sometimes contain additional drawings or sketches of explanation where there is a difficult point. Both these suppliers produce perfectly adequate drawings for modellers although the reproduction cannot obviously quite meet the standard of magazines and other expensive publications.

Bellona, with their range of Military Vehicle Data, provide good photographs but only two-view drawings, ie front and side, though if you have some drawing skill the top view can be drawn up to give the complete picture, though you may have to resort to a little bit of guesswork for the rear unless you have suitable photographs as a guide. Photographs are, however, obtainable from M. P. Conniford, 12 Westdene Crescent, Caversham, Reading, Berks, who has a long and detailed list. Pictures are, of course, also obtainable from the Imperial War Museum. *Airfix Magazine* also regularly features drawings and complete construction articles, some old issues of which are available from the back-issues department.

I think the most useful reference book to have is *The Observer's Fighting Vehicles Directory,* by Bart H. Vanderveen, published by Frederick Warne & Co Ltd. This gives nice potted descriptions as captions to the photographs and covers about 900 vehicles with additional text on history, classes and variations. Two others by Chris Ellis with colour artwork by D. Bishop are *Military Transport of World War I* and *Military Transport of World War II,* published by Blandford in their 'Mechanised Warfare

Above: A selection of wheels available from Airfix kits, reading from left to right they are: Scammel Tractor, Bedford QL, Land Rover; Tank transporter trailer, German Armoured Car 234, American Half-track trailer; AEC Matador Refueller, 25 pdr Quad Tractor, 88 mm Flak Gun and, finally, one from the Austin in the Emergency set.

Below top: Coles Crane mounted on a Thornycroft chassis ready for painting. Note the jib from Microstrip, door hinges and handles made from stretched sprue, and the mudguards adapted from the Austin Fire Tender.
Below bottom: The Thornycroft Amazon Coles Crane completed and finished in khaki.

in Colour' series. Almarks also publish several useful little books of which *British Military Markings 1939-45,* and *Wehrmacht Divisional Signs 1938-45* are particularly valuable. If you can't afford to buy a lot of these order them from your local library and also check their catalogues for others—my short list is only of those books I find particularly useful.

We now come to the actual construction work which can be broken down into the three basic sections of chassis, bonnet/cab and bodywork.

Chassis

In a lot of conversion projects the basic chassis will be available from one of the Airfix range of kits, possibly by shortening or extending, so explore these possibilities first. There are a host of conversions using the Austin K3 and K6 in the Emergency Set alone, for example the Austin K3/YF, the K6/ZB and many other 6 × 4 vehicles having a similar wheelbase. If you cannot find a suitable chassis complete, then you at least require a set of wheels of correct diameter and width. Here the range is even more extensive, from the Scammell Tank Transporter to the Land-Rover and trailer in the Bloodhound Missile Kit or even the little Jeep. Old Matchbox and Corgi Junior diecast will often yield a set of the right size and even a tank kit offers solid-tyred wheels suitable for early types of motor truck. While we are discussing wheels there are ways in which these can, indeed must, be altered. You will find when making vehicles other than those of British manufacture that although the size may be correct the centres will not look right. However, we can either adapt centres from another kit or build them up with discs or inserts. To give some idea of how this can be done refer to the photographs of the Russian GAZ and the sketches showing how these are cut and 'domed' on page 15. These wheels were from the Emergency Set but the diameter was reduced by sandpapering carefully.

Chassis side frames can be drawn or traced on to plastic card from the working drawings and here you may find it easier to cut four from 30 thou plastic sandwiched together in pairs though if you have 60 thou card available by all means use it. Build up the chassis keeping square with cross members where appropriate, and when dry you can add the springs and axles though it's usually better to leave them until the cab and body have been added, as it is then simpler to line them up. The various sketches on the next page show the type of construction and the important point is that the chassis must be built square and level otherwise the body and cab sections will never sit right.

Cab/bonnet

It is fortunate that the majority of military vehicles are of a very simple shape and thus their reproduction in miniature is not too difficult. The beginner should first try his hand at conversions using kit cabs like the Austins previously mentioned, then as he gets used to working in plastic card more elaborate constructions can be attempted. A reasonably accurate Bedford OX or OY type cab and bonnet can be made from the Austin K6 Fire Tender and this is a good introduction to cab building. First cement together parts 28, 29, 31 and 33 (after plugging and removing the hip ring) and then saw off the complete bonnet when dry. Also cement together parts 23, 24, 25 and 26, add the steering column and wheel and paint all the inside. Join together the cab and mudguard sections then when dry sand off the square edges of the mudguards before constructing the simple bonnet as shown in the sketch. Driving mirrors can easily be added with an arm of stretched sprue and the mirror head from either a punched disc or, if rectangular, a short length of thin Microstrip.

Forward control cabs like the Crossley Q types or Thorneycroft Nubian are relatively simple structures and can almost invariably be based on the mudguard section from the Austins, Bedford QL or the AEC Matador, being built up as shown in the sketch. If they cannot be based on any kit mudguard section, fit a rectangular floor and mould the mudguards as

Right: *Styles of 'open' or soft top cabs, left to right: Ford (Canadian) Anti-Tank Gun Portee, Guy FBAX and Austin K3/YF. Note how the microstrip proved too fragile for the tilt frame on the Ford, this would be better replaced with plastic rod.*

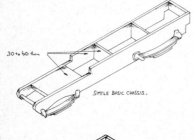

30 to 60 thou.

SIMPLE BASIC CHASSIS.

described earlier, fitting these neatly underneath. Of even simpler form are the topless or soft top style cab like the Guy FBAX or the Canadian Military Pattern Cab No 43 as here you have no problems of window frames or roofs.

However, the vast majority of military vehicles, and this applies especially to German vehicles, are of the cab and bonnet type and this is the kind we shall have to master. These fall naturally into two parts for construction, a boxy cab, with or without windows and roof, and an engine compartment or bonnet. If these are built to a common floor, lining up should be simplified and the sketches again show some ideas. Get into the habit of taking measurements from the drawings, allowing for the

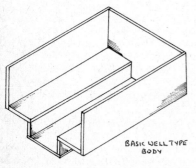

BASIC WELL TYPE BODY

Exploded view of Bedford OY showing construction detail. A scale plan of this vehicle appears on page 16.

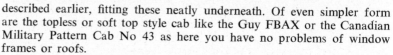

20 or 30 thou.

SUPERFINE MICROSTRIP

40 thou.

2 x 30 thou.

20 thou.

MODIFIED AUSTIN CAB

USE AUSTIN FIRE TENDER CHASSIS CUT SHORT AT REAR.

20 thou.

NYLON MESH

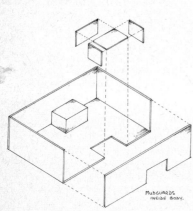

MUDGUARDS INSIDE BODY.

Exploded view of a truck body of the recessed rear wheel type showing method for obtaining mudguards.

Construction details for two types of basic military vehicle cabs.

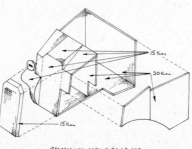

15 thou.

20 thou.

15 thou.

CANADIAN MILITARY TYPE 43 CAB.

60 thou.

20 thou.

30 thou.

20 thou.

60 thou.

THORNEYCROFT TYPE CAB

Above: *GAZ AA truck under construction showing opened bonnet with simple engine and open cab door.*

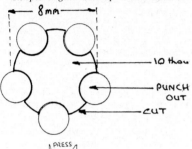

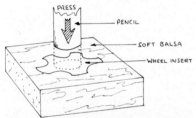

The two diagrams above show how to achieve the domed shape necessary for the GAZ truck conversion described in the text.

Above top: *Russian GAZ AA 6 × 4 truck showing much modified wheels.* Above bottom: *GAZ AA 4 × 2. Not an easy model to build but with the addition of a few figures will make up into a nice diorama piece.*

thickness of adjoining parts where applicable, and drawing these parts direct on to the plastic card. In particular note that on a tapering bonnet the length of the sides should be taken from the plan (ie, top) view as to measure it from the side view would mean the resultant parts would be too short. Constant checking back to the drawing is essential as is careful measuring and marking out, with a 'dry run' assembly before final cementing together at each stage.

Bodywork

The bodywork is normally the simplest part of the model but it must be square and true. The floor should be made from at least 20 thou plastic card. If it's a long body then use 30 thou. The sides, depending again on the dimensions, should also be from 20 thou. As an example we'll take a simple wooden body, say for the OY Bedford. Mark out the floor, including lines of planking, and then score this in with the point of the compass. Hold this vertically, and against the steel rule of course, but don't press too heavily otherwise the parts will bow when cut out. Just persuade the point to gouge out the lines. Mark out all the sides in one long strip and plank them all in one go, both sides of course, and don't forget to allow for the ends to go between the sides.

Next cut out the sides and join together with little slips of Sellotape round each corner and then fit the floor inside, flush to the bottom. When all is to your satisfaction, brush Mek-Pak into the joins. Cross members can be added from Microstrip, if applicable, as can the body ironwork after first impressing any bolt heads gently with the compass point. Some early British vehicles were fitted with a well-type floor which, instead of being flat, had the centre portion recessed between the chassis runners as shown in the sketch. Provision will also have to be made in some instances for rear wheel mudguards to project into the body, but this is usually quite simple to arrange as all it entails is building a box inside the main body. Both these types are shown on the opposite page.

House type bodies are again quite straightforward. Always cut out window apertures and score in panel and door lines, etc, before cutting out the parts; internal partitions are often of use to avoid 'sag' or distortion in long types of body.

Tilt hoops can be made from plastic rod bent round a warmed steel knitting needle, though this rod can sometimes be persuaded to stay bent without any application of heat. I have even used split bamboo for these frames and this can also be bent in the heat of a candle flame. Canvas hoods can be depicted from toilet tissue well crumpled up to make it more flexible. It will stick to the hoops with cement or Mek-Pak.

We should be at the stage now when we can assemble the main components, the bonnet/cab and the body, to the chassis frame. This should again be done with care to see that the parts are true with each other. You can add the springs and axles, slipping on the wheels temporarily to ensure that the model sits square or in the chosen attitude. The wheels, springs and axles will normally be available from one of your 'cannibalised' Airfix kits, but if you are stuck use a cocktail stick, either wooden or plastic. The axles and springs are seldom visible when the model is finished. When these are all dry remove the wheels as they will want painting separately, of course.

We now come to the detail finishing and these little additions will make or mar your model. Start with the larger pieces first, such as the tool boxes, fuel tanks, steps, rear mudguards or flaps, where these are not part of the body, and again you will find suitable items in Airfix kits. If not they are quite simple to fabricate from card, Microstrip, rod and plastic scraps. Door hinges and handles can be cut from stretched sprue, as can wiper blades if you have glazed the windscreen.

Now is the stage where study of photographs will come in useful for such extras as petrol cans, spare wheels, tarpaulins, tow ropes and all the

Above top to bottom: Component parts for the Bedford OY; Underside of model before fitting wheels; Finished model, note the 'lift' at the front as the vehicle strains to pull up a tricky slope. Model is mounted on simple rectangle of hardboard with the 'landscape' from plaster and a crew taken from other kits.

multitude of gear that is loaded aboard military vehicles. Some of these can be made at home, for example Jerricans, usually carried somewhere, can be moulded by using one from a tank kit or the American half-track as a master. Cement securely a sprue handle to the back of one of these and impress this 'can' into a slab of soft Plasticine leaving an impression behind as a mould. Now mix up enough Plastic Padding to fill the impressions and smooth it well into each, leaving to dry for about 15 minutes. The Plasticine can be peeled away, the moulded 'cans' cleaned up and sanded to trim off the flash. I have used this method to make spare wheels and other parts of simple shape where it was too expensive to 'rob' a kit. If you have trouble with the 'master' sticking, a thin film of liquid soap in the Plasticine mould should cure that. Of course, this simple moulding leaves an impression on one side only, but for wheels and cans where only one side shows, this is sufficient.

Last job of all is painting, though sometimes it is best to do some of this as you go along, otherwise certain parts can be difficult to get at. I now find that painting the chassis and under parts with a darker shade of the main colour (ie, by mixing in some matt black) sets off the model better. This darker shade can also be used in door panel lines, round bonnet openings, etc, to give a bit of depth to those parts. Mud or dust weathering can add highlights to mudguard edges, and the underside of fuel tanks, but again your study of photographs will show where, and experience will show how. Diorama work allows great scope for the vehicle to be painted in with its setting when shadows and weathering can be accented accordingly. Wheels, as I have mentioned before, should be painted separately on the end of a wooden cocktail stick, and tyres in a dark grey look better than in black. Humbrol Panzer Grey is about right for tyres and these should be painted first. The wheel centres, in the main vehicle colour, are done last, picking out any nuts with a darker shade, and then weathering the rims and tyre treads as necessary.

The drawings reproduced here will give you one or two simple conversions to work on with a few of a more complex nature for use as you gain experience. I hope the photographs of my models will also show not only some of my 'successes' but also some of the failures and mistakes. There's nothing like the cold eye of a camera lens for revealing your errors.

Modelling military vehicles is a subject with almost limitless prototypes and variations; in fact if you were to make one every week for ten years you wouldn't have made half of the types used in World War 2!

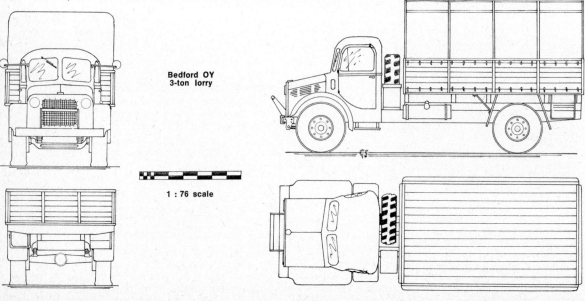

Bedford OY
3-ton lorry

1 : 76 scale

OUTDOOR MODEL RAILWAYS

By Bert Lamkin

ONE THING which most model railway enthusiasts need is space, and in modern houses this is in short supply. If you wish you had room for a model railway layout, how about taking a look in the garden if no indoor nook or cranny is available to you? And even if you already have a nice indoor layout and feel the need for new adventures in model railways, stay with us and consider the prospects.

Garden railways have long been one of the more exotic branches of model railways and the term usually conjures up an image of clockwork or live steam models, possibly vintage tinplate items, chugging along exquisitely laid (and expensive) track in huge country or suburban gardens: a vision of the 1930s rather than the 1970s, in fact. With that the embryo garden railway modeller simultaneously conjures up visions of large sums of money and quietly forgets the whole matter. However, this *is* 1972 and if you make the best use of the model equipment which is in the shops now the possibilities are endless and the cost need be little more than that needed for 00/HO layouts—it could even be less.

Above: *An LGB narrow gauge train on temporary laid track to illustrate how a natural bank can easily be cut into to provide a rail bed. Some tidying of the grass has yet to be done. The proximity of the path gives access to the track.* **Above right:** *O-gauge train in Santa Fe livery manufactured under the Atlas trademark by Roco, the Minitanks people.*

Take a trip to a large model railway stockist now and you'll find a surprising number of different modern Gauge 0 and Gauge 1 models ready to run and refreshingly inexpensive even by 00/HO gauge standards. The secret is plastic combined with the huge North American and European markets which means long run production, in gauge 0, at relatively modest prices. There are three major manufacturers, Rivarossi (sold under the AHM label in America), Atlas and Pola-Maxi. The first two make ranges of American-style equipment, with Rivarossi also making European (Italian and German) models. Pola-Maxi make a range of German outline models only. A British firm, Three-Aitch, make a range of neat British outline freight wagons, all in kit form similar to Airfix 00 wagons, and there are quite a number of accessory items like cast metal water towers also on sale to match gauge 0.

Some of the equipment mentioned is shown in the accompanying photographs. Locomotive prices start at a little under £6 for the Plymouth industrial diesel in a variety of finishes, and around £10 for the Pola tank engine and the American diesel locomotives. More exotic locomotives, mainly of American types, cost around £30 ready-to-run though they can be purchased in kit form much more cheaply. This price is just about the upper limit for the new generation of plastic moulded 0 gauge models, and it is interesting to note that it is still way below the selling price of hand-made or limited production models of the more traditional sort; for these £47 to £50 is the cheapest price. Plastic moulded 0 gauge rolling stock is

Sketch A: *Construction details for an elevated track. Standard 2 inch × 2 inch posts are used for the uprights and 2 inches × 1 inch for the base. The T section method is to give rigidity. Posts may be spaced six to eight feet apart on straight runs. If ballast is to be used then retaining walls of hardboard or waterproof plywood strip are required.*

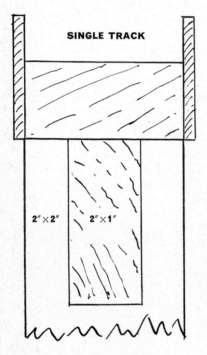

SINGLE TRACK

2″ × 2″   2″ × 1″

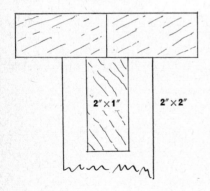

DOUBLE TRACK

2″ × 1″   2″ × 2″

also relatively inexpensive, mostly in the £1.60 to £2 range per item. To give just one example of outlay, the excellent Atlas F-9 diesel locomotive, a beautifully engineered model, and the four freight cars shown in the pictures cost just under £15. Substituting the little Plymouth industrial diesel would chop this figure by nearly £5 and still give you a good operating set of stock to get started. By all other 0 gauge standards, these are rock bottom prices to pay for top quality models which are built to fine scale standards.

The track situation is also extremely good. Peco make their well-known 'Streamline' track in flexible yard lengths in the 0 gauge size as well in the better known 00/HO and N gauges. Prices work out at under £1 a yard, and turn-outs are also available at just over £3 each. Rivarossi make a snap-together flat bottom track of American/European type which is sturdy, of fine scale appearance, and also modestly priced. Track to make a 5 feet diameter circle costs about £5—and a circle this size makes a good run. Straights and turn-outs come at comparable prices. Atlas make the cheapest track of all with turn-outs at only £1.60—little more than the 00/HO gauge price. The Atlas track, however, though sturdy, will not join with the other two makes though it could, no doubt, be made to do so by filing down the cross-section where it joins. The track section is actually deeper than the other makes, being to American 'toy train' standards.

All this is by way of showing what is available to anyone who contemplates a garden layout using the gauge 0 size. In passing I should just mention that there is a similar range available in Gauge 1 (1:32 scale) make by Marklin and comprising steam and diesel type locomotives, some coaches and wagons as well as track. Gauge 1 is an even more hallowed scale for garden railways. The Marklin prices work out more expensively than the smaller gauge 0 models. The steam tank engine model is £19, for instance, the most highly priced item in the range but still cheap by the standards of hand-made or vintage 'tinplate' models. All remarks I make here about constructing a garden layout apply equally to gauge 0 or gauge 1 models, however.

Now let us see what making a layout in the garden entails. The initial step, before making a garden layout, in common with full-size railways, is to become your own surveyor and civil engineer and assess how the terrain can best be used for the intended layout. If the garden has already been laid out by some dedicated member of the household, then some co-operation is obviously needed in routeing the line, but this need not be a stumbling block, the two interests can be quite compatible. If it is 'virgin soil' then one has considerably more scope. Your preliminary survey will note land slopes, trees and/or large shrubs, outbuildings, fences and paths of access, etc. The next stage is to produce a plan of the site to a suitable scale; be fairly accurate with this. One can now spend some very interesting hours determining how the new railway can fit into this plan.

Although the actual line is going to brave the weather, it is worthwhile to arrange for the terminus—or through station if it is to be continuous—to be under cover.

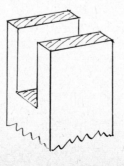

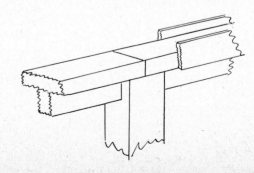

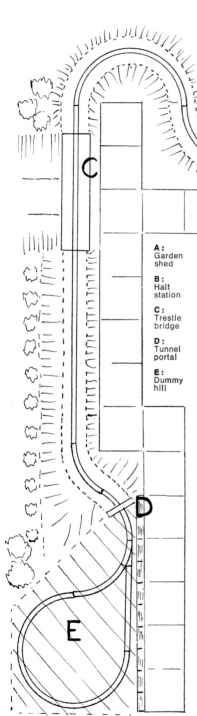

A:
Garden
shed

B:
Halt
station

C:
Trestle
bridge

D:
Tunnel
portal

E:
Dummy
hill

Sample plan showing a very simple arrangement of single track to give a continuous run. One reverse loop is situated in a garden shed, the other beneath an artificial hill. Access to the tunnel is by means of lift-off roof sections. The points are spring loaded and polarity is controlled from the shed.

Another aspect to consider is the scenic side. Indoors one endeavours to create a scaled model landscape—outdoors the scenery is completely oversize, so unless one aims at reproducing a miniature setting it is best to divorce the line from the surroundings. This can be achieved by elevating the track and, incidentally, making operation and maintenance easier. The height above ground is a matter of personal choice. Flexible Peco 'Streamline' track can be supported on quite a light timber construction. Sketch A shows two methods; materials to hand may dictate various modifications but if possible avoid having all the joints together on each section. The vertical supports for the curves are closer and must be rigid enough to form the plywood strips into the curve. The ends of all verticals should be well soaked in creosote or similar preservative before inserting into the ground and the whole structure given a good coat before any track laying.

In common with the prototype one has to consider drainage and expansion, to prevent the accumulation of water and provide for movement. The former is achieved if you are using the 'contained' method, by drilling a series of small holes through the base or retaining walls; the other method will drain itself.

With expansion, which can be considerable, the pinned track needs oversize holes in the sleepers and a small gap at the rail joints. In all cases these joints need bonding with short lengths of wire if you plan to electrify the line. If you use ballast instead of pins or screws, then this will allow for track movement; occasionally, as in full-size practice, a certain amount of re-aligning will be required.

Periodically wiping the rail surface with an oily rag will maintain a good pick-up surface for electrical operation; too much and you'll get wheel-spin. I have used a petrol additive known as Redex for this, and this is a very useful liquid for preventing corrosion on non-weatherproof surfaces. With 'Streamline' track the radius of curves can be increased with advantage using the extra space available, and sketch B gives one idea for supporting bends in the line. Again there are various ways and the builder may have something stowed away that is just the job.

I mentioned bonding across the rail joints, ideally soldered all the way, but as this is usually impractical then small plugs and sockets are the answer, soldering one end of the wire to the rail before installing. The strips of connectors obtainable from electrical shops are possibly the cheapest as they can easily be cut into singles, or pairs, as required. A spot of paint over the soldered joint and adhesive tape round the other connection will help to prevent corrosion. Of course, two things common to both indoor and outdoor layouts are a firm base for the track and good electrical conductivity.

With the track elevated one can avoid severe gradients or almost eliminate them—a well-known railway engineer endeavoured to do this in full-size—in the interest of good running. Keep the initial layout fairly

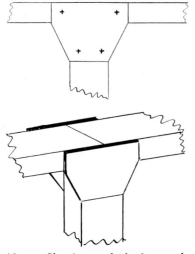

Above: *Showing method of strengthening supports with hardboard or plywood sides.*

Some of the Atlas 0-gauge stock from Roco. From top to bottom, an F-9 EMD 'covered wagon' diesel finished in Santa Fe livery; a 40 foot box car with sliding doors; a 50 foot gondola; and a 'steel' type caboose. These models are ideal for use with Peco 'bull-head' type track, but the wheel flanges will need some filing down if they are to be used with Rivarossi track.

simple but allow enough room on the supporting structure to expand. Model railways do not have to remain static and after the first season in the 'great outdoors' some developments will undoubtedly take place.

If you feel apprehensive about the line during the worst of the weather it can be covered with plastic sheet, but do not forget to put a tie round to stop the wind lifting it.

With both gauge 0 and gauge 1 the easier alternative to an elevated line is one at ground level, making use of the natural surroundings and using suitable 'scale' plants for trackside foliage. Although 7 mm scale can still be dwarfed by the average garden plant, one can arrange for only the smaller varieties to be adjacent to the railway. This is definitely a case of co-operation with the resident gardener!

On the ground, the natural hazards will need coping with and the prepared plan should have the elevations marked, so the line can either avoid or cut through 'hills' — low lying areas, that is; any that are habitually flooded should be by-passed or bridged over. A firm road bed must be established, removing turf and weeds. A spray of weed killer along the route will check these—grass especially can be a menace. The lay of the land will site cuttings and embankments and the banks of these must not be liable to landslide by being too steep or loose. With cuttings, a small channel at the foot running parallel with the line is an advantage. A length of 3 × 3 inch or 3 × 2 inch timber about 18 to 24 inches long with a suitable handle is useful here—a substitute for the steam roller!

Apart from the usual gardener's tools of trowels, etc, a good spirit level is a necessity. It is all too easy to create a 1 in 20 gradient if you rely upon the eye alone. The transition from level to grade must be gentle and even, with no sudden rises and dips. The same adage applies here as in everything—do not rush things.

If there is to be a tunnel, and it is a good thing for the train to disappear from sight on any layout, then the walls and roof must be strong enough to prevent caving in if stood upon. An earthenware drain-pipe can be just the thing. Make sure the diameter is large enough. If it is on the big side the entrance and exit can be masked with suitable portals. The track is pinned to battens running along the pipe. These, being at the ends of the sleepers, will keep the track central by virtue of the curve of the pipe, the space below providing drainage.

The nickel-silver plastic sleeper rail produced in 0 gauge by Peco will save a lot of maintenance. Needless to say, the amount of traffic on the line will govern the extent of cleaning needs. Make sure that all bridgework and tunnels are secure on their site—you don't want a bridge slewing under the impact of a shower of rain. Not until all these points are taken care of is the track laid. If you are using electric traction, rail joints must be bonded with solder and also one or two feeder cables must be run to the more distant sections. These want to be fairly heavy gauge—Ohm's law will show that when using low voltages the resistance must be kept to a minimum. Ordinary rail joiners, as used indoors, will be inadequate.

The track can be ballasted in a similar fashion to the prototype. It wants to be about $1\frac{1}{2}$ inches deep with the sleepers bedded into it; you will need the spirit level again for this process. As the loading gauge starts at rail level the depth of the ballast must be allowed for on any overstructure. For ballast, there are several sources: the finer shingle on some beaches, crushed granite used for certain tennis courts, the local builder's yard or, of course, your local model shop. It is better to have ballast too coarse than too fine. Too fine ballast will allow dirt to collect and so spoil the drainage, hence sand is unsuitable. Of course with exceptionally heavy rain you may get some ballast washed out of place— but this happens in full-size.

If the line is left unused for long periods then tunnel mouths should be sealed against habitation by small mammals! Clearing an obstruction in the middle of a normal tunnel can be quite an exercise. Although we

Top: *Laying Lytag pellet ballast for LGB track.* **Below:** *The finished track laid on the levelled road bed. Odd pieces of tile or paving slab are used to retain loose soil.*

are dealing with twice the size of 00 models the housing of complicated pointwork and rolling stock under cover should be considered—somewhere to retreat to for that sudden shower.

So far we have been considering electric railways, but for those who do not want to get involved in electrical circuits outdoors, there is still the Triang-Hornby 'Big Big' train system. This is really aimed at the toy market and is designed for young children. However, for our purposes the range includes a very neat Hymek diesel locomotive which needs little more than a repaint to be a fine scale model. The 'Big Big' train system uses torch batteries carried inside the model to provide self-contained electric power. There is a neat little diesel shunter, overscale but convertible, and a steam type locomotive which only needs a new home-built body to be ready for the road on an 0 gauge layout. Using these locomotives your prices are virtually halved as they are cheaper than 00/HO gauge models. The track does not need to be electrified so the problem of power feeds and bonding is dispensed with. Most toy shops sell 'Big Big' train equipment and the range includes a few wagons and coaches too. 'Big Big' train models run happily on the Peco 'Streamline' track.

As I've already hinted, it is best to keep garden railway track plans very simple. A sample plan is shown which actually illustrates the LGB layout I am building in my garden. It is just as suitable for gauge 1 or gauge 0. It will be noted, however, that it features two return loops which need special wiring to prevent short circuits. If you have any model railway experience—or books on the subject—you'll know what to do about it. Suffice to say we cannot go into this in detail here. With the 'Big Big' train system there is no wiring involved, however. An alternative would be an end-to-end layout with the main terminus in the shed (A) and a country terminus at (B), possibly under a canopy. Each terminus could feature a run-round loop with, possibly, a storage siding as well. Terminus (A), under cover, could certainly include this feature, possibly with other sidings as well.

Quite apart from the conventional methods of making outdoor road-beds, already described and shown in the drawings, there is a more recent idea which at least one modeller uses very successfully. This involves the utilisation of plastic moulded rain guttering to hold the entire track bed. The lengths of track are tacked to longitudinal creosoted wood battens. The plastic guttering (made by Marley among other firms) is laid in a shallow trench, having had drainage holes drilled in it at about 5 inch intervals. The guttering is filled with shingle or gravel until just about an inch from the top. The track (on its battens) is laid along the guttering, and the gravel or shingle ballast is then laid up to the normal level and tamped well down. Like real track the model track is left free-standing. Arthur North, of Birmingham, who first showed this system to me, has had a large oval layout in his garden for well over two years with no appreciable movement in the free-standing track. He runs heavy steam locomotives on his track, not the rather lighter modern electric types. Where the track rises above the natural level of the garden, the guttering

Right: *This type of track is excellent for 0-gauge outdoor railways. Made in the CCW range, the rail is brass and the sleepers (ties) are plastic. It is sold for simple home assembly complete with spikes, and is stocked by the largest model railway suppliers. The track is best made up on wooden laths as shown, the laths holding the track firmly in the ballast.*

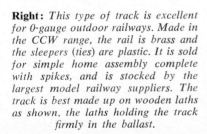

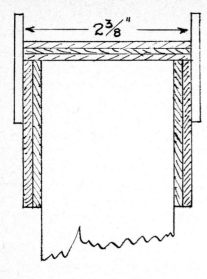

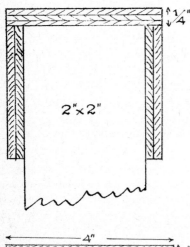

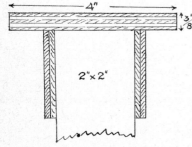

Sketch B: *Standard 2 inch × 2 inch timber is again used for the uprights, but the radius of the curve determines their spacing. Intermediate blocks help to support the track base. This can be quarter inch waterproof ply for single track or ⅜ inch for double track. Sides are laminated for ease of construction and ultimate strength. Attach the inner strip to the posts first, using glue and panel pins for the plywood strips and screws to fix to the posts.*

is supported on stakes, with screws through the bottom of the guttering. The stakes are creosoted. An embankment is then built up to the guttering with plenty of rubble, then earth, and grassed over. For curves the guttering is sawn into short lengths—from a foot or longer—depending on track radius, the adjacent sections being butted together and joined with the joiner sections supplied with the plastic guttering systems. Most hardware shops and builders' suppliers sell plastic rain guttering quite cheaply. This method also works with gauge 1 or LGB track.

Narrow gauge

My previous remarks have been based upon the assumption that the constructor would be following standard gauge practice, but one can adopt narrow gauge procedure if desired, with its somewhat simpler approach. With the advent of the German LGB system, narrow gauge in the garden presents a completely new picture. Built to 1:22 scale the stock is large enough to hold its own in the plant world. In fact in this size the garden really becomes an adjunct to the railway and as it will negotiate two foot radius curves the possibilities are endless.

For the novice wishing to get going quickly on a garden railway project, the LGB system almost commends itself for first choice. With overall price to be considered, it is possible to get a modest LGB layout in operation for around £30. This may sound expensive, but for your money you can get a small diesel or tramway locomotive, two or three wagons, and an oval of track; some 0 gauge locomotives cost more than this for the engine alone. Spending a little more money you can get a small steam-type locomotive, an excellent model of a Krauss 0-4-0, while a splendid 0-6-2T of the Austrian Zillertalbahn is available for anyone with £25 or so to spend on a locomotive alone. The small diesel or tramway locomotives at about £12 each are a better choice to get you started, however. LGB is the nearest a lot of people will ever get to owning a big railway and it is certainly pleasant to operate. The wagons and coaches are big and chunky, they make the same sort of creaks and squeaks as the real thing, and all the details, like doors and latches, really work. Plastic moulding of very high quality is used throughout, and the workmanship and engineering is superb. The strength of each model is remarkable and wagons and locomotives take hard knocks with seeming impunity. Locomotives have a sealed maintenance-free mechanism with a smooth wide speed range and no parts exposed to dirt or dust. Miniature driver figures are supplied with the locomotives and there is a wide range of accessories. In Britain LGB is sold by the Beatties chain of model shops in London, Leeds, and Manchester.

The track is of the snap-together sectional type like a giant version of the sort sold in 00/HO gauge train sets. Substantial rail joiners and clips ensure a positive connection and so long as your layout in the garden is fairly small and in a sheltered position you should be able to get away without bonding the connections at all. Brass rail is supplied but this is quite expensive at £1.80 a length (1972 price), so a cheaper aluminium type is also sold. This cannot be used outdoors as it oxidises too quickly. However, I've found that this problem can be overcome by painting the entire rail in matt brown 'rust' colour, then wiping just the top surface clean. When the track is in position wipe the unpainted running surfaces with a rag full of Redex motor oil. This stops the oxidising and if anything enhances the conductivity of the rail. Make this Redex application a regular fortnightly chore.

One great feature with the LGB system is its portability which enables you to have the best of both worlds. An outdoor layout can be set up on the lawn for almost any period from a complete day to a complete summer and the track can be taken up again after this period, cleaned off and put away until required again. As the track snaps together so simply, dismantling even a large layout takes no more than 30 minutes. It is even better if you can move off the lawn to a site elsewhere in the

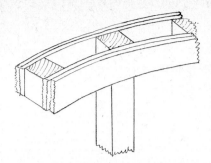

Above: *Showing laminated sides and intermediate spacing blocks in a curve.*

garden. Chris Ellis did this most successfully last summer in a roughly 10 foot square corner of his garden. Here he dug a trackbed with spade and trowel, dropped down gravel 'ballast', fitted in the track as an oval with a couple of sidings, and used rocks, bricks and soil to build up temporary scenic features. The track stayed down for the latter half of the school holiday period, ie, August and early September, when there were several neighbourhood youngsters to operate it. As fine weather predominated there was little effect on the track. For operating sessions the locomotive and wagons were taken outside and a normal power unit was used on an extension cable from the house.

Obviously, if you try this idea for yourself, choose a well-drained site, not a corner which becomes waterlogged in the rain. To prevent track 'creep' spike the track sections with a nail every few feet. It is necessary to watch grades but with LGB the laying of the trackage is nothing like so critical as it is with 0 gauge in the garden. In fact, a temporary LGB layout has full-size narrow gauge precedents. Contractors' lines in the old days were usually put together on site using prefabricated track lengths, as were the military narrow gauge lines on the Western Front, 1914-18. The idea in both cases, of course, allowed for the site to be moved when operations went elsewhere.

Above: *A short section of 0-gauge track laid in a section of plastic guttering. This is sunk into the ground, partly filled with coarse ballast and covered with a layer of finer ballast (usually small grade shingle) on top of which the track is bedded. The gutter retains the ballast in position.*

Right: *Another view of the Atlas 0-gauge train running across an as-yet very bare terrain.*

In contrast to all this, I have myself laid a complete LGB system in my own garden on a permanent footing. This follows exactly the procedure suggested for gauge 0, with respect to laying permanent track. Because the brass or aluminium track can be expensive, when bought in the large quantities required for big outdoor layouts, Beatties sell straight lengths by the yard with the plastic sleeper sections separate. The rail is a steel or aluminium alloy and needs the paint and oil treatment previously mentioned to prevent corrosion. The aluminium rail cannot be soldered when it is bonded together on outdoor layouts and the answer here is to drill through the web of the rail section and bolt fishplates across the join in full-size fashion. An alternative would be to bind wire through the holes to join adjacent sections. A special aluminium solder is available but this is difficult to use unless you've had experience of this sort of work. LGB track is similar in section to some brands of 'glide' type curtain railing and it is therefore possible to buy this material (preferably in brass) and make your own track by spiking it to sleepers in the traditional fashion.

However, if you lack the sort of skills necessary for this type of work, my advice is stick with the conventional LGB brass track even if it means building the layout in short sections as funds allow.

For ballasting on my permanent LGB layout (which uses a mixture of all the track types mentioned here) I use Lytag, a mineral pellet which looks right for the job. Other point to remember with LGB is that the ordinary 1 inch square wood timber sold in hardware shops is a scale 2 ft square in LGB size, ideal for trestle bridges and other engineering work.

THE AVRO MANCHESTER

By Alan W. Hall

THE AVRO MANCHESTER was not one of Avro's more successful aircraft but from it sprang the Lancaster which did much to hasten the end of World War 2. Thoroughly disliked by air and ground crews alike, the Manchester was one of the RAF's biggest disappointments in the early years of the war. Its failure was due in no small part to the unreliability of the Rolls-Royce Vulture engines which were the weak link in an otherwise successful chain. The aircraft, although it entered service with more than eight RAF and Commonwealth squadrons, spent more time in development than it did on operations. Its story, however, is important, for from the Manchester came the immortal Lancaster, Britain's key aircraft in the bomber offensive of 1942-45.

Secret Development

During the expansion of the RAF, which started in mid-1934, considerable reliance was placed on the Specification B13/36 which called for a twin-engined bomber carrying a maximum of 12,000 lb of bombs and having the capability of dropping torpedoes. Much thought was given to the original requirements and it even went as far as providing resting quarters for the crew. The first Manchesters off the production line actually had folding spring beds but these were soon removed because of weight limitations.

Several firms tendered designs for the specification and Handley Page and A. V. Roe's were selected to build prototypes. Eventually the Handley Page HP56 was dropped in favour of the Avro 679 which eventually became the Manchester, and within weeks of ordering the prototype a production order was placed for 200 aircraft to a new standard written around Specification B19/37. Avro built a wooden mock-up at their Newton Heath factory and it was decided that the Metropolitan Vickers plant could also produce the aircraft in quantity. The engines offered by Rolls-Royce were, in fact, 'double' power units which came about by building two Kestrels together in a common crankcase so that the unit had 24 cylinders in an 'X' configuration. The unorthodox engine was tried out on a Hawker Henley but even at this early stage it proved troublesome and there was an obvious need for a lengthy testing period.

Below top: View showing the radiator shape of the Vulture engines and giving a good dead front view of the Manchester. Below bottom: The first prototype Manchester L7246 seen at the time of its first flight from Ringway on July 24 1939. It was later used as an instructional airframe with the serial 3422M (Imperial War Museum).

Above: *The Manchester prototype L7246 seen at RAE Farnborough during the feasability trials of the bomber catapult. The aircraft was mounted on a trolley with the tail supported by a 'V' shaped rear mounting to keep the correct flying attitude whilst being shot down the catapult runway (MoD PE).*

First Flight

The prototype Manchester L7246 took to the air on July 25 1939, piloted by Captain H. A. Brown. It was obvious from this 17-minute test that the Vulture engines were not giving the power calculated and with a high wing loading it made the aircraft difficult to fly. Later the wing was extended by ten feet to give a 90 ft span.

First flights were conducted in great secrecy, and no mention appeared in the press. Shortly after the beginning of the war the prototype Manchester went to A & AEE Boscombe Down for service evaluation, but because of reports of instability on the initial flights it later went to Farnborough for aerodynamic testing. To counter some of the flight problems a central fin was added to the rear fuselage making the Manchester a distinctive shape for the spotters. Later this fin was modified and eventually the tail unit was redesigned so that the aircraft had only twin fins and rudders similar to those on the Lancaster.

Into service

Following the fall of France the aircraft industry went into top gear to produce fighters at the time of the Battle of Britain. The impetus given to production meant that the bomber force, too, were provided with more aircraft to carry on offensive operations. The Manchester was hurried into service after two prototypes had flown, even though these had many teething troubles and were the subject of a mountainous list of modifications before they could be sent to squadrons.

No 207 Squadron at RAF Waddington was the first to be equipped. L7278 and L7279 arrived on November 10 1940, after having been quickly

Right: *The second prototype Manchester which was the first armed version. Serialled L7247, it too became an instructional airframe after completing its test flying (Imperial War Museum).*

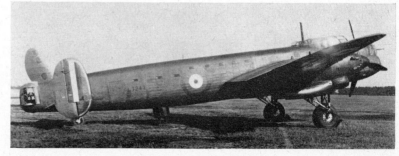

The Avro Manchester

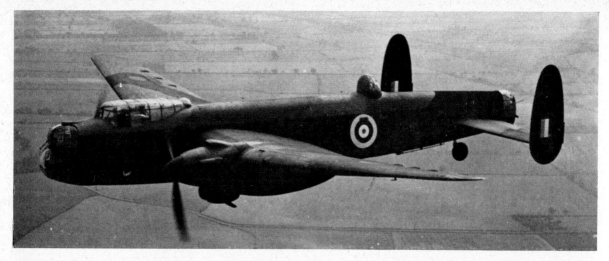

Above: *Manchester Ia, L7486, shown without squadron markings; it served with both No 207 Squadron coded 'P' and then No 50 Squadron. The aircraft was written off in a landing accident at Skellingthorpe on March 25 1942. Note the wider span tailplane and the larger fins and rudders which served as prototypes for the Lancaster tail assembly* (Imperial War Museum).

processed through No 6 Maintenance Unit at Brize Norton. These were extensively flown throughout the month to complete 500 flying hours during which time Rolls-Royce representatives supervised engine maintenance. Another aircraft arrived before the end of November and the build-up of the squadron started.

The existence of the Manchester was revealed by the RAF in January 1941, but only limited information was given. No 207's first operation was against a 'Hipper' class cruiser which was reported at Brest and, together with 30 aircraft detailed from No 3 Group and 25 Hampdens from No 5 Group, six Manchesters of the squadron took part. All returned safely but one had to force land at Boscombe Down through engine oil covering the windscreen. Another crashed on landing back at Waddington due to a failure of the hydraulic system.

There followed many months of planning raids, plus some suspended operations due to mechanical faults. Several new squadrons, including Nos 97, 49, 50, 61, 83 and 106, were formed, but few saw any length of service. Raids were made on the Kiel shipyards, Cologne, and other industrial targets in Germany, and one Manchester even succeeded in reaching Berlin, dropping five 1,000 lb bombs, three 250 lb bombs and a packet of leaflets.

Another catastrophic operation happened on June 22 1941 when aircraft of No 207 Squadron were detailed to attack Boulogne. Shortly after take-off one Manchester was shot down by a Beaufighter of No 25 Squadron, which had been alerted by ground controllers to an enemy intruder aircraft flying in the area. All seven of the crew were killed. At about the same time a Defiant attacked another Manchester of No 97 Squadron within three miles of its home base. Other aircraft on the raid returned with engines blazing and the hydraulic system causing difficulties.

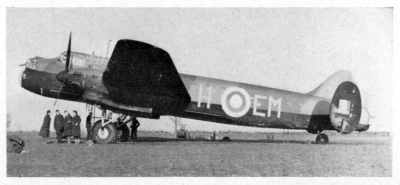

Right: *This Manchester, L7288, served with Nos 207, 97 and 61 Squadrons before going to No 1654 Conversion Flight Waddington* (Imperial War Museum).

Above: Fitting the new balsa outer wing panels to the cut down Lancaster wings. **Above right:** *The new engines in place after final shaping are given a coat of filler.*

Later other problems showed up, such as tail flutter when the aircraft was climbing on full load and the erratic behaviour of the feathering units of the propellers.

The Manchester crews flew their aircraft never really knowing whether the engines would let them down at a critical moment. One of Bomber Command's Victoria Crosses was won by Flying Officer L. T. Manser who, flying L7301 on the night of May 30 1942 at 7,000 ft over Mannheim, made his bombing run in spite of intense anti-aircraft fire. The Manchester was repeatedly hit and crew members injured as the pilot set course for home. One of the engines overheated and Flying Officer Manser found that the aircraft was down to 1,000 ft, and likely to lose more height. By carefully nursing his remaining engine he climbed steadily but before long it was obvious that the crew had to bail out. Several of the crew members got away but Manser, although he had a parachute, stayed with the aircraft until it was too late to get out. The Manchester stalled into the ground and burst into flames.

Several interesting experiments were tried with Manchesters at the Royal Aircraft Establishment at Farnborough. One included catapulting the aircraft with full bomb load in a series of experiments early in the war designed to do away with long vulnerable concrete runways which were found necessary with the increased all-up weight of the bomber force. Weighing 37,000 lb, Manchester L7246 was literally hurled into the air, and the feasibility of launching bombers in this manner proved. Unfortunately the project lapsed as changing operational conditions meant that runways were no longer as vulnerable as previously thought.

Another experiment took Farnborough scientists in the opposite direction. Due to the number of incidents of Manchesters overshooting the runway, generally because pilots preferred a high-speed landing to eliminate the chance of a stall on the approach, it was decided to devise an arrester gear so that the Manchester could be brought to a halt without difficulty. The tests proved that from 72 mph at touchdown the Manchester could be stopped in 460 yards. Although 120 sets of arrester gear were ordered for various airfields in 1942, the idea, as with the catapult, lapsed.

End of operations

In June 1942 the Manchester was withdrawn from operations. There was, however, no question of scrapping them as there were now so many available. They were all relegated to training duties and most of them found their way to Bomber Command Conversion Units. Needless to say, the Manchester was hardly suitable for pilot training but it was said that once you could fly a Manchester the Lancaster was a 'piece of cake'.

Manchester conversion

To change the Airfix Lancaster kit into a Manchester is a major job. Not only does one have to make a four-engined bomber into a twin-engined one, but almost every other part of the original kit is affected, with the exception of the fuselage length—and that alters slightly if you count the odd few scale inches involved in rubbing down the bomb aimer's

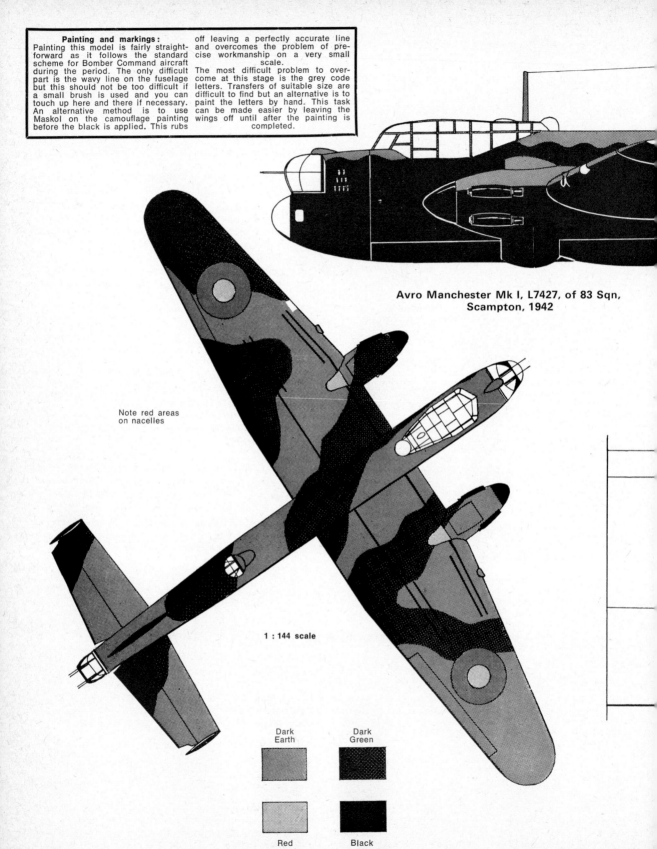

Avro Manchester Mk I, L7427, of 83 Sqn, Scampton, 1942

Note red areas on nacelles

1 : 144 scale

Dark Earth

Dark Green

Red

Black

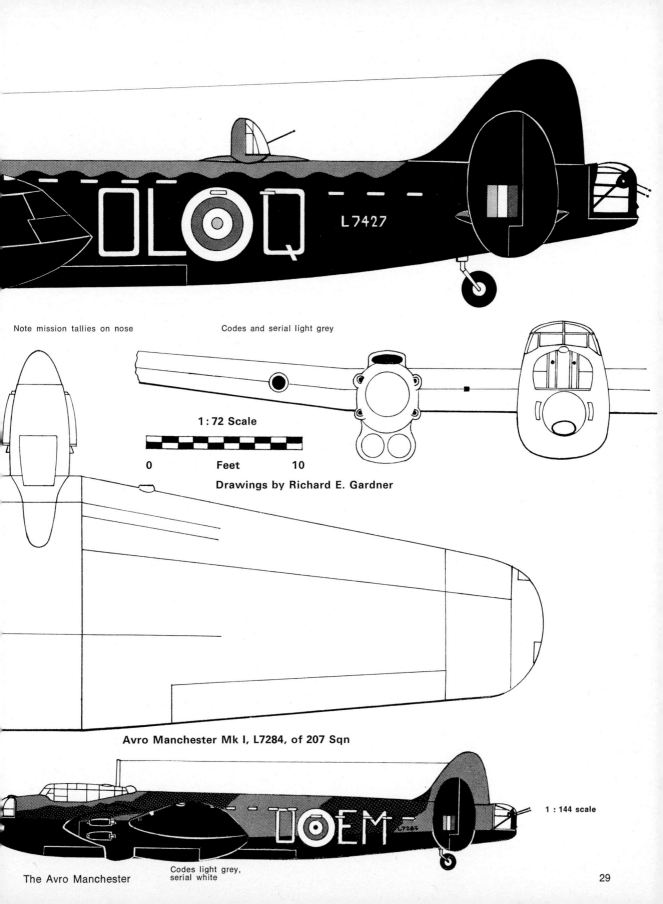

Note mission tallies on nose

Codes and serial light grey

1 : 72 Scale

0   **Feet**   10

Drawings by Richard E. Gardner

Avro Manchester Mk I, L7284, of 207 Sqn

1 : 144 scale

The Avro Manchester

Codes light grey,
serial white

Above: *Mid-upper turret assembly; hole drilled in fuselage balsa block with a Stirling turret ready for fitting.*
Above right: *Close-up of central fin after cementing in place.*

canopy! The complete task from start to finish took me 58 hours, or three weeks of evening and weekend work.

The work in most cases is not too difficult but it is time-consuming. Most is spent in rubbing down wooden parts, painting and making new canopies. Luckily I found that the work could be split up into several distinct sections, which was very convenient as it was possible to work on one whilst other parts were drying out or cement was setting. The secret I found was to keep the wings separate from the fuselage until the model was virtually complete. Some modellers may even wish to leave the wings out of the slots altogether as the model will pack away into a smaller space if these are not stuck in place. The original wing-to-fuselage joint is an excellent one, as those who have already made up the Airfix Lancaster kit will agree. The port wing in particular is a perfect fit and slots into the position easily every time. The starboard side is a little slacker and tends to be rather sloppy to start with, but the application of several coats of paint on the joint makes the fit easier.

As the work of converting the Lancaster can be divided into various sections, I have divided my description under the appropriate headings. The order in which these parts are tackled is up to the individual.

Fuselage: This is perhaps the easiest of the various parts, as luckily the fuselage length of the Manchester was exactly the same as the Lancaster apart from a few inches difference in the bomb aimer's window on the nose. After having assembled the cockpit detail and added the nose turret, the two fuselage halves are stuck together and set aside to dry.

I removed the Lancaster mid-upper turret fairings completely by cutting away a rectangular section $1\frac{1}{2}$ inches long and of sufficient depth to clear the lower part of the fairing. A balsa wood plug is added, which when dried out is shaped to the rest of the fuselage section. A liberal coating of clear dope and talcum powder filler is applied and the whole section rubbed down until the joint lines are clean. At the same time it is worth removing some of the rather heavy detailing on the fuselage as this will also be removed from the wings during their preparation, and it looks odd to see one part of the model with heavy surface detail and the rest without.

At this stage modellers may wish to leave the Frazer Nash turret off as in the drawing, but the construction of the turret represents no real problem and does add to the final finish of the model. The turret used was left over from a Stirling C Mk V transport conversion. This was assembled on its base with the guns in position. The lower rim of the mounting was removed and a hole in the fuselage balsa block cut out. To do this I used a coarse bit in the drill to get most of the required area away and then finished with sandpaper. With luck you will find you have located the hole exactly over the mounting of the Lancaster turret which is left in the fuselage and the new turret will slot into position with ease. Some Manchesters had low fairings in front and behind the turret and these can be made from plastic wood or from scrap plastic and sanded into shape before the turret is stuck in place.

Wings: Both wing halves are assembled as for the Lancaster. I debated whether or not to cut the outer wing panels off altogether or try to reshape them. Time dictated that the former course was the best and I therefore removed the outer panels at the start of the dihedral line.

The outer panels were cut from $\frac{1}{2}$ inch thick balsa plank. A tracing from the plan was used to transfer the shape and this was traced down on to the balsa through carbon paper.

A 1 inch chisel was used to carve most of the wing cross-section and then the remainder was taken down, firstly with coarse sandpaper, and finally with well worn 'wet and dry' paper. The dihedral angle at the root of the new wing was dealt with carefully as both wings had to match in dihedral angle. To do this I rubbed the aerofoil section shape down by sandpaper, frequently comparing the results against the plastic part of the wing and in turn against the other side. The wooden and plastic parts are joined, the whole given several coats of filler and rubbed down thoroughly until a perfect finish is achieved. The two halves of each of the Lancaster ailerons are assembled and their leading edges rubbed down to fit the shape of the ailerons for the Manchester. By scribing round their outlines when in position on the wing, I was able to cut out neat slots for each by using a very sharp knife. Each aileron is then stuck into position.

A position for the landing light is cut out in a similar manner from the port wing; the actual transparency will be dealt with later and it is worth keeping the piece of wood removed as this can be used as a former for moulding the landing light.

Circular wing air intakes just outboard of the engines are next considered. Here I used pieces of dowel rod cut into a V shape at one end with the actual circular hole drilled in the other. By cutting a similar shaped V in the right position on the wing I was able to slot the intakes into position and then after having applied a liberal amount of filler regained the wing leading edge shape with the intake nicely fitted into position. A careful study of available photographs is of value here to see the exact shape that these intakes require.

Before leaving the wings I took care to see that the wing slots accepted the wing at the fuselage joint and found that slight filling was necessary on one side.

Engine nacelles: Like the outer wings these, too, have to be made from wood. I made them from three pieces of balsa, partly pre-shaped before their addition to the remains of the Lancaster's inner Merlin engine nacelle which is stuck in place on the wing after that part of the construction is complete. The three parts consist of the main engine nacelle and the upper and lower radiators. After having cut the plastic nacelle away at the leading edge of the wing, a piece of balsa is stuck in place which lines up with the top of the plastic, leaving room for the lower radiator to be put in place underneath it. Both parts *must* be cut roughly to shape before cementing them to the nacelle stub, otherwise the engine cannot be properly shaped. The upper radiator is also pre-shaped—its

Below: The completed model ready for painting. Canopy has been placed in position for the picture but is not cemented on until after painting. All wooden parts must be velvet smooth using dope/talcum filler, mixture and sanding as described in previous articles in Airfix Magazine. Below right: Completed model depicting a machine of 106 Squadron.

Above: *Manchester I, L7284, in No 207 Squadron markings. It was issued to No 61 Squadron in April 1941, later went to No 39 MU and was struck off charge in June 1943.*

outline is first cut from balsa sheet and the intake hollowed out. It is then stuck down and the nacelle finally finished. The lower radiator has two holes drilled in the front before shaping begins. The outline can then safely be finished off without fear of damage to the remainder. Care must be taken in finishing to match the diameter of the spinner to the cross-section of the nacelle. The former is not stuck in place until a coating of filler has been applied and rubbed down. Exhausts, two on each side of the nacelle, are filed from scrap plastic and added before the final coat of filler is applied.

The undercarriage of the Lancaster suits that of the Manchester. The wheels of the latter were slightly smaller than those of the Lancaster but the difference is so minute that one need not bother to rub down the kit wheels before putting them into place.

Tail unit: The Manchester's tail plane in the triple fin version is 5 feet less in span than that of the Lancaster. It is fairly easy to cut this unwanted piece from the kit tailplane after having measured off the required distance from the plan. The locating tab naturally has to go in this surgery but there should be no difficulty in cementing the revised tailplane back in position. During the cleaning up operations I also reduced the size of rivet detail on this section to conform with the rest of the model.

The central fin has to be made from balsa wood. For this I took a piece of $\frac{1}{8}$ inch sheet and after having placed the shape from the plan cut out the outline and then obtained the aerodynamic shape with sandpaper. As the fin is of fairly light construction I did not consider it necessary to cut and slot it in to the top of the fuselage and preferred to cement it in place with polystyrene cement. When complete the entire fin was given a thick coating of filler which was sanded down before being ready for painting.

The outer fins and rudders were taken from the Lancaster kit but cut down considerably. Most of the top of the fin is removed by a saw cut and the remainder of the unwanted area carved away with a knife; files and wet and dry paper are used to give the final shape.

Transparencies: The mid upper and front turrets have been dealt with already in this conversion. Most attention has to be given to the cockpit canopy which has to have the kit canopy's astrodome removed with a fine toothed saw. The dome is then sanded down until it is lower than the original and the whole cemented back in place when the rest of the canopy is stuck to the model.

Before doing this a radio aerial is cut from plastic card and a hole of suitable size drilled in the roof of the canopy. By using a file I was able to lengthen the hole into a slot which took the aerial satisfactorily. The drilled hole went right through to the top of the fuselage and the aerial was notched so that this provided a secure foundation for the whole assembly. The two side blisters are added after the transparency has been located in position on the model. To do this I held each in the tweezers and painted a thin outer line round the edge using an old thin brush and liquid polystyrene cement.

Next comes the bomb aimer's transparency. This is not so deep as that of the Lancaster; consequently it has to be rubbed down before assembly. The area around the nose to which it is cemented can also be rubbed down slightly so as to make the fit accurate.

The rear turret which has a shape all of its own will have to be moulded. Firstly a former or male mould has to be shaped to fit the requirements. This is finished with a filler and sanded down before moulding can start. The female mould is also cut from obechi sheet and I moulded the turret after the style already described in several articles in *Airfix Magazine*. Similarly the port wing landing light has to be moulded but here you can use the wood cut away when the wing was dealt with, so there is no need to make another mould. If you do not want to mould a new rear turret it is just possible to use a discarded Lancaster dorsal turret turned on its end. The gun slots need to be extended, however, and the whole transparency must be repolished after being worked on.

A NOSTALGIC LOOK AT THE EARLY DAYS OF KITS

By Fred Henderson

Above: *A Skybirds kit box, in this case containing a model DH80 Puss Moth, the parts of which are shown in front of the box.* **Above right:** *The kit parts for another Skybirds model, the Blackburn Shark; engine and wheels were cast metal, and struts were stamped metal.* **Far right:** *A Skybirds Walrus stands in front of the famous Skybirds wooden hangar which had sliding doors. In the foreground is another Skybirds accessory, the six-wheeled petrol bowser. Skybirds 1:72 scale mechanics can also be seen.*

IT IS NOW about 20 years since the first plastic kits, as we know them, appeared on the model market and a large number of readers of this book probably cannot remember the time when plastic kits were not readily available. The older ones amongst us can do so, however, and it is interesting to recall the earlier pre-plastic kit days and how the modellers then, smaller in numbers but every bit as keen, used to produce their models. Before plastic kits appeared there was not the variety of subjects that there is today, and the kit market was dominated by aircraft. I do not propose to consider the flying-scale aspect but only the non-flying or, as we generally used to call them, the 'solids'. They mostly were just that, carved from solid wood, although built-up balsa wood and card models had a loyal band of devotees. Card modelling has recently shown signs of revival with the availability of printed sheets from Germany to add to the limited number available here previously. This form of modelling seems to have maintained its popularity in Germany, even though it has declined somewhat in Britain. Built-up balsa wood construction nowadays is confined to flying models but back in the 1930s it was used to produce very detailed exhibition models, of which more later.

Many modellers in the pre-war period scorned the use of kits (as, indeed, some do even nowadays) but kits were bound to evolve as a natural answer to a demand which, although limited, was to grow steadily. By the early years of World War 2, model kit production had become a considerable industry.

In the early and mid 1930s, interest was almost exclusively in aircraft and ships, the latter, other than large working models, being mostly water-

Right: *A 1:24 scale Bristol Bulldog made up by the author from an Aero-models kit and photographed by him in about 1930.*

line with 100 feet to 1 inch as the most popular scale. Adequate information was available in books and plans to provide sufficient detail for the small-scale models. Cars were not a popular modelling subject then and no kits were produced pre-war; the earliest kits I can remember were a series of racing and sports cars by the Scale Model Equipment Co which appeared soon after the war, around 1946. Their kits had solid wood bodies, partly shaped, with metal wheels and fittings and rubber tyres, the scale being 1:32. It happened that some of the earliest plastic kits were cars in the same scale, the Highway Pioneers by Gowland & Gowland produced around 1950 in the United States of America. This 1:32 scale for cars has remained the most common. Military vehicles, apart from the diecast Dinky Toys range, were a much later eventuality; the problems involved in making the wheels and tracks were an obvious deterrent to scratch-builders, or kit producers for that matter. Skybirds included some cast lead alloy military vehicles in their 1:72 scale range and this was about the nearest thing there was to models for military enthusiasts.

The obtaining of accurate information for modelling pre-war was always difficult, publications being limited in number even for aircraft subjects. We had *Flight* and *The Aeroplane,* of course, but they were 6d (2½p) a copy weekly, and that was a big sum to come from a schoolboy's pocket money in those days!

When the first Skybirds kit, the DH80 Puss Moth, appeared, it was quite a revelation although I remember having to run a lot of extra errands to earn enough to save up the price of 1s 6d (7½p). At that time, though we did not realise it, James Hay Stevens, who designed the Skybirds range, was originating what was to become in time the most popular of all aircraft model scales, the now universally accepted 1:72. Skybirds deservedly went from strength to strength, increasing in popularity as they widened their range. The presentation was attractive, a flat cardboard box, illustrated by a line drawing with a loose sheet of card inside to which were attached, with thread, the various parts. Fuselages and wings were of hardwood, partly shaped, tail surfaces were celluloid (later fibre was used), struts were brass wire or, later, stamped aluminium and wheels were either turned from brass or cast in metal. The early kits fell far short of perfection from the accuracy point of view and concessions, such as making the wings of the Puss Moth in one piece instead of separately, were made, probably to simplify manufacture. However, as techniques improved and sales grew, many refinements were introduced and the range was extended to include even such large types as the Handley-Page Heyford bomber and the Armstrong-Whitworth Atalanta airliner. They never did get around to providing cabin windows for the civil aircraft but we were quite content to paint them on to the solid wood. The military aircraft types mostly had open cockpits (pre-drilled into the fuselages) and with the closed-cockpit types canopies were provided. A Skybirds Club was formed with a regular magazine, adding much to the interest, and articles on conversions were as popular as they still are today. As time went on many accessories and figures were produced, even hangars!

In the United States of America solid models were popular but 1:72 scale was practically unknown. Drawings in magazines such as the *Model Airplane News* (a predominantly flying-model orientated publication) when they appeared were either to 1:64 or 1:48 scales, the latter being easily the most popular for solid modellers in the USA. Aircraft and Hawk (still well known in the plastic kit field) were two firms producing kits in 1:48 scale, the former using balsa wood and the latter hardwood. Diecast and stamped metal fittings were utilised by both firms. Some specialist dealers in Britain imported these kits and they were much prized by enthusiasts! I particularly recall building an FE2B from an Aircraft kit and regarding it as something of an achievement with its multiplicity of bamboo struts and thread rigging, not to mention the hundreds of bits of thread stuck on to the wings and tail to represent the ribs.

The most popular range of built-up card models was produced by Aeromodels in Cheshire and I well remember the excitement, having saved up for a kit, of waiting for it to arrive by post. Prices were from about 2s 6d (12½p) to 5s (25p) each, quite expensive for the time, and they were not generally available from local shops so had to be ordered by mail. To a scale of ½ inch to 1 foot (1:24) these large models were very accurate and remarkably well designed and highly detailed (the modern Airfix 1:24 scale kits give an idea of size). The range, starting with a DH60, Gipsy II Moth, was eventually to include, amongst others, the Sopwith Camel, Bristol Bulldog, Gloster Gauntlet, Hawker Hart, Supermarine S6B, Comper Swift, Puss Moth, Fox Moth and largest of all, the DH84 Dragon, almost two feet wing span! Folding wings were provided where appropriate (a blessing from the storage point of view) and interiors were fully detailed with opening doors for the cabins. Construction was straightforward, adequate instructions being provided, also *full-size* drawings in most cases, and the completed models were very robust. The parts were printed in black outline on white card and all painting, including markings, had to be done by the modeller, no transfers being provided. A complementary Aeromodels range of similar construction but to 1:48 scale appeared eventually but was never as popular as the larger models.

I mentioned earlier that I would return to the subject of built-up scale aircraft made with balsa wood, a method used mainly for flying models. Usually the so-called flying-scale models of the period were little more than freelance designs having only a superficial resemblance to the prototype which they claimed to represent but one notable exception amongst manufacturers was the American Cleveland company. Their kits were really first rate, the parts being clearly printed on high grade balsa sheet whilst the full-size construction drawing was a masterpiece; the scale again was 1:24. The design provided for alternative versions, either a rubber-powered flying model with simplified construction and enlarged prop and tail surfaces, or a true scale model with full structure giving rib, spar, former and stringer spacing as for the full-size aircraft. Control surfaces

Right: *A manufacturer's publicity photograph of a 1:24 scale Hawker Hind from the Sweeten's range. This finely detailed model could be made up as a flying or non flying model, in the latter case with a scale propeller as shown here.*

A Nostalgic Look at the Early Days of Kits

Top: *A Gloster Gauntlet from the Aeromodel range.* **Above:** *A Fairchild 91 built from an Aircraft balsa kit.*

Right: *One of the original Frog 'Penguin' plastic models, a Short Singapore III flying boat in 1:72 scale was released in 1937, one of the first-ever plastic kits. The fine hangar and slipway in the picture were accessories in the 'Penguin' range.*

were hinged and almost unlimited detail could be added by the modeller to produce a fine exhibition piece. They were not quick or easy to build but they were really worth the effort. The range included the popular American fighters of the period such as the Curtiss P-6E and Boeing P-12/F4B series as well as many civilian types such as the Waco Custom, Lockheed Vega and even the twin-engined Electra.

I have no recollection of any kits being made on the Continent pre-war, although most European countries had a strong following for flying models. At least one firm in Britain, Sweeten's of Liverpool, produced a small range of high quality flying scale kits, something in the Cleveland manner, but I never built any of these. Most British modellers tended to combine flying and non-flying modelling activities, the latter being mainly a winter pastime because most summer evenings we spent repairing the ravages of the previous weekend's flying or designing and building that flying masterpiece (or monstrosity as the case may be) destined hopefully to win the coveted Wakefield Trophy. We struggled gamely with formulae and experimented with folding props and retractable undercarriages; as often as not the model was a flop but who cared? It was all good clean fun!

Back to the subject of solid model kits I must mention those made by Chingford Model Aerodrome, appearing shortly before the war and continuing right through it. They were to 1:48 scale, some in hardwood, some in balsa and a three-view blueprint was included with each kit. The wood parts were partly shaped and the early kits did not provide cockpit canopies although these did appear later.

In the late 1930s came the advent of the first plastic kits, the Penguin series by Frog. By that time 1:72 scale was well established so it was natural that it should be chosen for the new kits. Presentation was similar to that of the Skybird kits but with mouldings which had simply to be cemented together (balsa cement was used). These kits were deservedly popular at the time and are, indeed, still sought after today by many collectors but they did not, as might have been expected, spell the end of wooden kits. In fact balsa solid kits by Veron (who seems to have been the last manufacturer in Britain) were on sale in post-war years long after the Penguins had gone off the market. Veron balsa kits included such 'modern' types as the Wyvern and Sabre. The Penguin kits were made from an early type of acetate plastic which was, unfortunately, prone to serious warping, a problem which was not overcome until the introduction of polystyrene plastic kits many years later. The Penguin range was very extensive during the 1937-39 and early war period and some of the kits were re-issued together with new types after the war, but they were not available for very long. Most of the well-known World War 2 aircraft were produced, such as the Spitfire, Hurricane, Blenheim, Battle, Hampden and Wellington, to name only a few, but they also included some less likely types such as the Monospar ST25 Universal Ambulance and the Short Empire flying boat and, perhaps the best of all, the Short Singapore III flying boat, a massive biplane and very impressive indeed as a model. Transparent canopies were included and details such as radial engines were very neatly moulded and would compare well with many present-day parts. So we link up with the polystyrene plastic kit but that is another story and a very big one indeed.

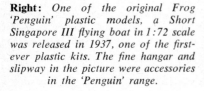

RADAR IN THE ROYAL NAVY

By Peter Hodges

Guns, torpedoes, missiles, boats and so on are all familiar items of equipment to ship modellers, and most enthusiasts know all about them. Much less familiar—sometimes barely visible—are the radar aerials and their attendant displays and systems. With modellers very much in mind, Peter Hodges here tells the story of naval radar and describes and illustrates the principal Royal Navy systems.

AS EARLY AS 1935, the British government was considering the problem of defence against air attack from the continent of Europe, where increasing numbers of bomber aircraft were being built. It would be impractical to provide 'round the clock' fighter patrols over our vulnerable coastline, but if some 'early warning' system could be evolved, our fighter squadrons could remain grounded until an attack developed, and only then be committed to action. In this way, not only would precious combat engine-hours be saved, but also equally precious fuel, all brought to the United Kingdom by sea.

At about this time, Mr Watson Watt (later Sir Robert Watson Watt) was conducting experiments using electromagnetic beams to determine the height of the Gonosphere, and it seemed likely that these principles could be used to detect aircraft. Certainly, it had been noticed that the presence of aeroplanes near the television apparatus of the day often caused a 'double image' effect, and this was thought to be some sort of reflection from the 'planes themselves.

The outcome of all these deliberations was the chain of radar stations on the South Coast which played such a vital part in the Battle of Britain.

The potentialities of this Radio Direction Finding—or 'RDF' as it was then called—were immediately apparent to the Royal Navy, but a shipboard installation presented many problems. The new equipment would have to be squeezed into ships where space was already at a premium; and the designers had to take into account other special factors, such as field of view and aerial shape—remembering always the inevitable topweight penalties. However, the nettle was firmly grasped by HM Signal School, although much preliminary and time-consuming work was required on the design of the thermionic valves to suit a ship environment.

Development: air warning sets for large ships
TYPE 79

Naturally enough, protection was first sought for the larger and more important units of the Fleet, which were in any case best suited to take extra equipment and top weight. The first sea-going set was known as Type 79 and was already at sea in 1939 in the battleship *Rodney* and the cruiser *Sheffield*, with a further 30-odd sets on order. In passing, it is interesting to note that the Germans also had radar at sea at this time. The pocket battleship *Graf Spee* had a large aerial on the forward face of her main armament Aloft Control Tower—presumably an elementary gunnery set.

The Gunnery Branch of the RN itself quickly realised the enormous advantages of radar for gunnery ranging, because its only instrument was the optical rangefinder. Obviously, the range-taker manning it needed to see the target and there were therefore severe limitations in its use at night, in bad visibility, or against aircraft in cloud.

Above top: The Type 274 radar can be seen by anyone making a trip to the Tower of London as this is mounted on HMS *Belfast* which is moored close by as a floating museum.
Above bottom: The fore mast from aft. Radars are 293 cheese on platform, 974 navigation cheese on offset platform and 278 height finder centrally below. Although none of these installations are operational today they serve as a useful guide for anyone wanting to model the radar carried by British warships since 1945.

A *79B and 279B, with co-axial IFF 'pitchfork'*

B *281B, with co-axial IFF 'candelabra'*

C *271 within 'lantern'*

D *273 within 'lantern'*

E *277*

F *286M*

G *286P and 291*

H *293*

I *241 IFF 'pitchfork' with stabilising wind-vane*

J *242 IFF (fixed)*

K *242 IFF and 253 IFF (fixed)*

L *243 IFF 'candelabra'*

Above: *A view of the main mast on HMS Belfast with the post-war 960 warning radar aerial. Note its design compared with 281 in drawing B at right. Also of interest are the U/VHF radio aerials suspended from the lattice work either side of the mast.*

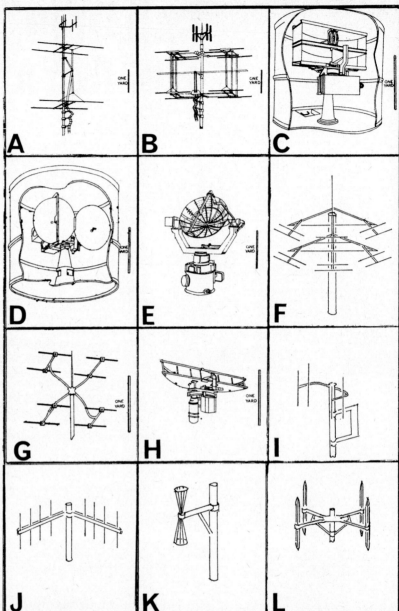

TYPE 279

The next development was a modified form of Type 79, known as Type 279, which had a ranging panel incorporated so that gunnery ranges could be transmitted from it. But there were now clashing requirements, for by allocating the radar to a specific gunnery target and holding it on one bearing, its function as an all-round early warning device ceased. It was quite evident that separate gunnery radars were required, and when they had been developed, 279 reverted to its proper function as an early warning set.

TYPE 281

Meanwhile, the general cry was for a better set with greater range and improved bearing accuracy and Type 281 soon followed 279. The new set could detect an enemy battleship at 12 miles, or an aircraft flying at

Above top: Newcastle *after her post-war modernisation. The 6 inch DCT has 274 and both 277 and 293 are carried on the lattice foremast. Notice the Mark 6 director with its 275 'nacelles' and the 960 aerial on the mainmast.* **Above bottom:** *The fixed 'pigtrough' aerials of Radar type 284 are clearly visible on the 8 inch DCT in this view of the cruiser* Berwick. **Right:** *A wartime shot of the sloop* Hart, *with 285 on the R/F director, 272, the IFF 'pitchfork' above it, and 291 at the masthead. Notice also the tall TBS radio aerial.*

16,000 ft as far as 100 miles. Its enhanced 'surface' range also provided better cover against lower-flying planes.

TYPES 79B, 279B, and 281B

These three early sets—79, 279, and 281—all used twin aerials, one being the transmitter and the other the receiver. They were mounted on the fore and main topmasts and rotated in synchronism. This arrangement was difficult to implement in aircraft carriers where space for masts is always a problem (because of their 'Island' superstructure) so variants of all three sets were produced. They were distinguished by a letter 'B' as a suffix to the basic number, indicating that a single aerial fulfilled the duties of both receiver and transmitter. Other large ships took advantage of this and sometimes had two quite independent sets, but it was impossible to tell from their appearance whether, for example, a vessel had one Type 79 or two Type 79Bs. This is of little consequence to the model maker, of course, and all the aerials discussed so far were very similar in construction.

Combined warning sets

There was soon a call for a radar set for destroyers and small ships generally, but at first no set with an aerial system compatible with a small-ship fit, in terms of size and top weight, was available.

By chance, the crew of a 'Walrus' amphibian on the slipway at Lee-on-

A 283 on barrage directors
B 274 (stabilised) on DCT
C 277 surface warning
D 243 IFF
E 293 combined warning/gun direction
F 79B or 281B air warning
G 253 IFF
H 251 radar beacon
I 285 on HA director
J 282 on pom-pom directors

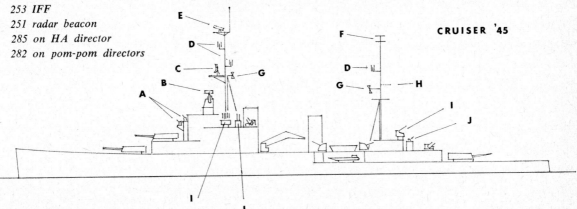

CRUISER '45

Solent noticed that its own small air-to-surface radar could detect the passage of shipping in the Solent. This led to the transfer of numbers of these sets from the RAF to the RN, where they formed a useful stop-gap.

TYPE 286M

In the Navy the set was called Type 286M and had a fixed 'bedstead' aerial on the fore topmast, facing forward. It could only give cover to about 60 degrees on each side of the bow and in any case the ship had to be swung to obtain even an approximate target bearing. Its range and accuracy were weak, and altogether it was unpopular because it imposed such severe tactical limitations on the ship carrying it. Even as large a reflective surface as a capital ship could not be detected beyond about seven miles.

TYPE 286P

To improve the capabilities of Type 286M, the aerial was redesigned to rotate and so give the much needed all-round sweep. In this form, the set was called Type 286P. It had been hoped that its range could also be improved, but despite the endeavours of the scientists ashore this did not materialise. The problems of the Type 286 series really stemmed from the fact that the basic set had not been designed in the first instance for warship installation, and suffered accordingly.

TYPE 291

Mindful of this, the backroom boys had already undertaken the research and development necessary to produce an adequate ship-borne radar. Their efforts resulted in the very successful Type 291. This could give accurate surface ranges up to ten miles with air cover out to 50 miles for high-flying aircraft. It was widely fitted in destroyers and small ships from about 1942—43 onwards, and survived into the 1950s.

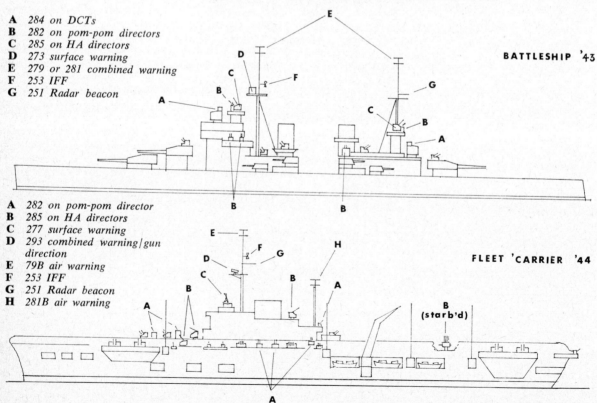

A 284 on DCTs
B 282 on pom-pom directors
C 285 on HA directors
D 273 surface warning
E 279 or 281 combined warning
F 253 IFF
G 251 Radar beacon

BATTLESHIP '43

A 282 on pom-pom director
B 285 on HA directors
C 277 surface warning
D 293 combined warning/gun direction
E 79B air warning
F 253 IFF
G 251 Radar beacon
H 281B air warning

FLEET 'CARRIER '44

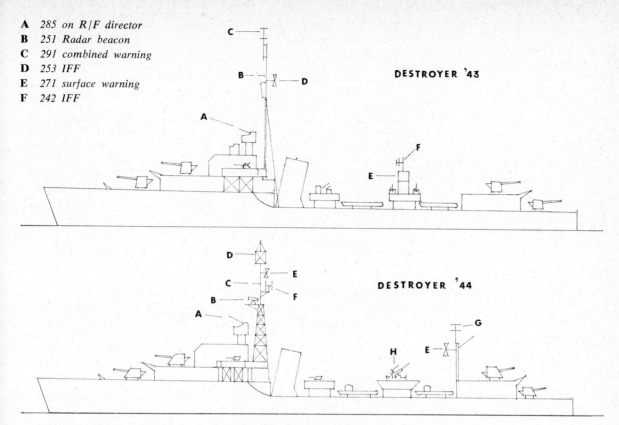

A 285 on R/F director
B 251 Radar beacon
C 291 combined warning
D 253 IFF
E 271 surface warning
F 242 IFF

DESTROYER '43

DESTROYER '44

A 285 on D/P R/F director
B 293 combined warning/gun direction
C 251 Radar beacon
D H/F D/F aerial
E 253 IFF
F 242 IFF
G 291 combined warning
H 282 on twin Bofors Mk IV (Hazemeyer)

Surface warning sets

Once the U-boat 'wolf-pack' tactics became established, whereby they shadowed convoys during daylight hours and made attacks on the surface at night (to say nothing of their habit of mustering their forces by radio when they surfaced), there was an increasingly urgent need for an efficient surface warning set for escorts. A U-boat on the surface escaped the probing beam of the Asdic and its low silhouette made it extremely difficult to detect visually. At night, therefore, it was virtually immune from detection.

Such a set was rapidly designed, to the great credit of those concerned, and was one of the major contributors to final victory. It was later discovered that this set was far in advance of anything that the enemy had, and the techniques involved were immediately passed to our American allies.

TYPE 271

The aerial for this outstanding set was contained in the now-familiar 'lantern', and the combination of short wave-length and high power output made it very efficient, even in such small vessels as corvettes. Its environment was then as low-set as could be imagined, yet a major surface unit could still be detected at about 12 miles and a surfaced U-boat at about three miles. The beam-width was of the order of five degrees, giving it a 'searchlight' form which greatly aided the bearing accuracy of the set as a whole.

The aerial and its associated 'office' were prefabricated in one piece, forming an integrated equipment. This was done to keep the length of the feeder cable (between the set and its aerial) to a minimum, for long cable-runs seriously dissipated the power output.

Type 271 was produced at very short notice, and was fitted in large numbers of Fleet and Escort destroyers as well as in smaller ships.

TYPE 272

A development of Type 271 was Type 272 which enabled the aerial and set to be separated by up to 40 feet, and the former could then be placed higher in those ships which could tolerate the top weight. The higher siting of the aerial much improved the range capabilities of the radar. The operator now trained the aerial (within its protective 'lantern') remotely, rather than directly as was the case with 271. In neither instance was a power training facility provided, but this at least allowed the operator to hold the aerial on any particular bearing when a suspicious echo appeared. The lanterns of 271 and 272 were almost identical, but while 271 invariably had an enclosed radar office immediately below it, 272 was mounted either on a special pylon, or sometimes on a platform on the foremast.

TYPE 273

Type 273 was an even more powerful variant, designed for capital ships and cruisers. Again, its aerial was housed in a lantern, mounted high on the main superstructure. So equipped, a battleship could detect a U-boat on the surface at over seven miles, and an opposing capital ship up to 20 miles away.

Gunnery radars

These were a natural development which released the original warning radars from their subsidiary task of providing gunnery ranges. The aerials associated with the sets were carried on the director or DCT, but an exception was the aerial array fitted directly to the Bofors Mk IV (Hazemeyer) mounting, which was 'self-contained' in the fire control sense.

TYPES 284 AND 285

Although the electronics of the first two gunnery sets were identical, their aerials were very different. For the control of surface fire in capital ships and cruisers Type 284 was used, its 'pig-trough'-shaped aerial being

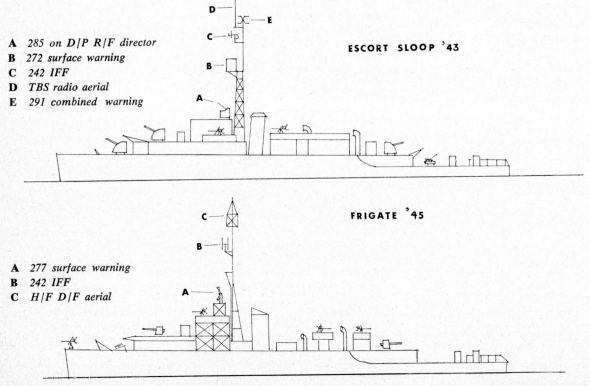

A 285 on D/P R/F director
B 272 surface warning
C 242 IFF
D TBS radio aerial
E 291 combined warning

ESCORT SLOOP '43

FRIGATE '45

A 277 surface warning
B 242 IFF
C H/F D/F aerial

Above top: The battleship Revenge *has 285 on both HACS directors, 273 in the mainmast 'lantern' and the double 79 or 279 aerials at each masthead.* **Above bottom:** *Close-up of the two HACS directors on the* Revenge.

fixed rigidly on to the appropriate DCT. Other than for corrections to allow for 'roll', the line-of-sight to a surface target was roughly horizontal, so there was no need for any elevation movement on the aerial itself. On the other hand, in High Angle Control System Directors and on the Dual Purpose Rangefinder Directors of small ships, it was necessary to elevate the aerial by some sort of take-off linkage coupled to the master sight drive. These small directors required a much lighter array, so a special aerial was designed—the familiar 'fish-bones'—when the set was called Type 285. It also had a small 'pig-trough' from which five, and later six, struts projected. The bearing accuracy of the set was reasonable, but its elevation accuracy was less good, so that while it could always be relied upon to range within a few yards, it could not be used to determine Angle of Sight and had to be 'aimed' at the target. It follows that it could not, therefore, be used in any form of 'Radar Lock-On' system.

TYPES 282 AND 283

Similar, but smaller, 'two-stick' aerials were developed for the Barrage Director (283), the Pom-pom Director (282), and the 'Hazemeyer' Bofors (282). The maximum range of these smaller sets was much less than that of their big brothers, but then they were only for use at close ranges. Type 284 was effective to a range of about 14 miles, while the lighter 285 could range on a large surface vessel at 10 miles or an aircraft at eight miles.

Later developments: combined warning sets
TYPE 293

This radar was originally intended to be a replacement for both 271 and 291 in small ships, but to give overall vertical cover between the horizontal and 70 degrees, its 'cheese' aerial was tipped upwards. This somewhat diminished its surface detection capabilities, but it was an excellent set for target indication purposes which became its principal function. It was this radar which put the individual gunnery radars on to selected targets and its aerial on a platform on the foremast became a familiar sight for many years.

TYPE 276

Another 'cheese'-shaped aerial of similar dimensions was linked to a set known as Type 276. It seems to have been interchangeable with 293, and occupied the same position.

TYPES 980 AND 981

In an attempt to overcome the difficulties of providing a truly combined warning set, Type 980 was developed for large ships. This had a double aerial, the lower part cheese-shaped to give surface cover and the upper part capable of independent movement in elevation. This upper aerial was particularly valuable as a height-finder but the mechanics of the array were complex and eventually the aerials were separated.

Height-finding was a very important element in the control of air defence, for by knowing the bearing, the range, *and* the height of an incoming raid, our fighters could be vectored by R/T to the most advantageous position.

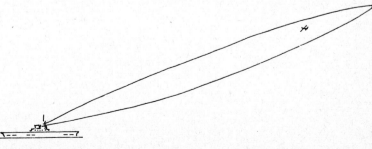

Right: *Typical side elevation of a height finder lobe. Range and angle of sight will be accurately measured, but bearing will be inaccurate.*

Radar in the Royal Navy

Surface warning

TYPE 277

An entirely new set, Type 277, was designed to replace the earlier 271/272/273 lanterns. Its aerial took the form of a paraboidal 'dish' which rotated continuously in power and could also elevate. The elevation drive permitted stabilisation in the vertical plane, but although in theory it could be used as a height-finder, when so employed the rotation had to be stopped on the required bearing. Again, one sees the problems which arise as soon as one set is used for other than its designed function. As a surface set, however, Type 277 was most efficient, with a bonus of being able to detect aircraft up to 5,000 feet out to nearly 20 miles.

Gunnery radars

TYPE 274

Capital ships and cruisers with DCTs had their earlier Type 284 replaced by the large 'cheese' aerial of radar Type 274. Again, there was no requirement to elevate the array, but it was later mounted in trunnion arms, to allow a stabilisation movement, so that it was unaffected by any ship movement along the Line of Sight to the target. The power follow-up of the stabilisation drive derived from a master gyroscope in the DCT itself which was also coupled to the director sights and the (now) secondary rangefinder.

TYPE 275

The greatest drawback of Type 285 lay in its inability accurately to measure angle of sight and, because of this, it could not be used for 'blind' follow. Its successor, Type 275, was accurate in both planes, and with this set full 'blind follow' against unseen targets was possible. The twin aerials resembled very large 'headlamps' and were set on each side of the HA/LA director. One aerial was the transmitter, the other the receiver, and both elevated in coincidence with the stabilised director sights. Type 275 arrived almost too late for World War 2 but later became the standard gunnery radar and is still in service in a few post-war ships.

Other radars :

Interrogator, friend or foe

An immediate problem arose when the first coastal warning radars came into service. The radar operators had no means of telling whether echoes were from enemy aircraft, or from our own planes, perhaps returning

Above top: *A typical Leander class frigate,* Arethusa *has 903 on her director, 976 on the forward face of the foremast, with 993 above and the H/F D/F aerial on the topmast. The shorter mainmast carries 965 with its own co-axial IFF.* **Above bottom:** *Close-up of the superstructure on* Arethusa.

Below left: *Plan and elevation of typical combined warning lobe. T 1, a high flying target, will be detected at range R 1 as the lobe sweeps through its position. Similarly, T 2 will be detected at range R 2. Target T 3, on the other hand, is a low flier and will not appear on the radar screen until it comes into the lobe. Target heights in all cases will be unknown.* **Below right:** *The narrow 'pencil' beam of a surface warning set, with good bearing accuracy.*

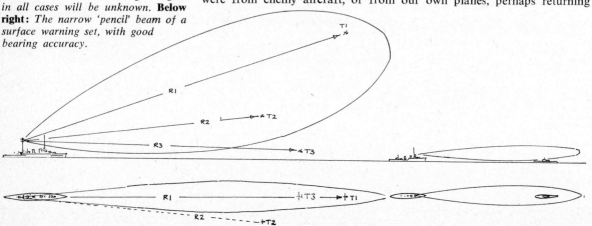

Above: *Rather unusually for a cruiser, HMS* Belfast *retained her after DCT. It, like its counterpart on the forward mast, had the stabilised 274 aerial in trunnions. This is just visible at the upper left-hand side of this picture.*

from a raid or for refuelling. To overcome this, the IFF set was evolved, entailing the fitting of a device in every Allied aircraft, so that when our radar 'looked' at it a characteristic shape of echo would appear on the radar display.

In order that the Interrogator 'looked' in the correct direction, its aerial had either to form part of the main radar aerial array, or had a quite independent rotatable system. Radars Type 271/272/273, for example, had a dipole IFF aerial projecting through the top of the lantern. Type 281 had a dipole aerial (similar in design to that of Type 291) attached to, and rotating with, the main array. The independent IFF aerial was a later development that trained automatically on to the bearing of a target picked up on the main warning set. It looked rather like a candelabra, and had its own platform, usually on the after side of the foremast.

Another Interrogator was used to establish friendly ships. Its aerials were fixed and resembled a pair of wire-mesh cones set vertically, point to point, carried on short struts projecting from the foremast.

Radar beacons

Yet another device was known as the radar beacon, which might be described as IFF in reverse; that is to say, it indicated friendly ships to Allied aircraft. Large warships carried it as a matter of course, but it was only fitted to a proportion of the smaller vessels. A typical selected ship might be that of the Senior Officer of an Atlantic Escort Group, on whom Coastal Command anti-submarine aircraft could 'home'. Like the ship-to-ship Interrogator, the radar beacon had a small fixed aerial, somewhere fairly high on the foremast.

Aerial characteristics

The radar transmissions from an aerial form a three-dimensional shape in the sky called a 'lobe', whose proportions are determined by several factors, which include the design of the aerial itself and the power output of the set. The aerials of the earliest sets were of the dipole type, rather like those of household television sets. In these, the 'poles' were set at a designed distance apart, the rearmost acting as a reflector for the other. This had the effect of directing the lobe along one axis, at the same time increasing the power of the transmission.

However, the most efficient form of 'reflector' is of paraboidal shape, like a car headlamp, and can be made to produce a probing cigar-shaped lobe, giving a high degree of positional accuracy at relatively short ranges. Most modern gunnery radars are of this type, and have characteristic 'dish' aerials.

The requirements of an air warning radar are to establish the range and bearing of a target as far away as possible and then to ascertain whether or not it is approaching. To achieve this, the lobe shape is modified so that it is of narrow width but of considerable depth and this gives high bearing accuracy.

One might imagine that a tall, narrow aerial would give this lobe shape, but in fact the contrary is the case, and it is produced by the 'cheese' design. This shape is, of course, simply a slice from a paraboidal contour and as we have seen the aerials of both 293 and 274 radars were like this. The 'fishbone' or 'Yagi' arrays, to give them their proper name, also developed the narrow-deep lobe. From the sketch on page 44 it will be seen that the range and the bearing of the two targets can be established but not their height and this is why radar 'lock-on' could not be achieved in the Type 285 system (see page 43).

In height-finding radars the exact converse applies. Now, the aerial is tall and narrow, or comparatively so, and its lobe is very shallow in depth but is of great width.

The lobe shapes can easily be demonstrated with an oriental fan. Flap it up and down and one has the height-finder; flap it from side to side and

Below: *Dipole principles. The reflector (r) helps to give the lobe direction and also strengthens the transmission. Without a reflector, the lobe becomes symmetrical about the aerial, but this is useful in such devices as Radar Beacons.*

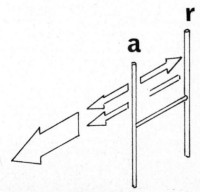

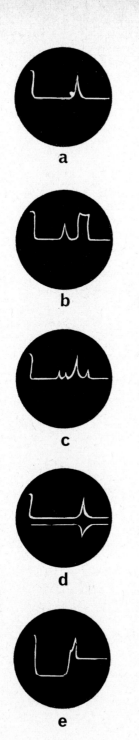

Above: *Five different types of radar displays*

a: Target echo 'strobed'

b: Echo and IFF return

c: Main echo with smaller target echoes

d: Echo with inverted ranging 'pip'

e: 'Stepped' trace

one has the air warning radar. Close the fan and one has the pencil beam of the modern gunnery tracking set. In passing it is worth mentioning that a radar specifically for surface cover can also have a lobe approaching the pencil-beam shape—like the 'lantern' sets, for example—because surface targets have virtually no height. But attempting to use, say, Type 277 for height-finding proved unsatisfactory, for as well as losing the all-round cover when the aerial rotation was stopped, it was extremely difficult to pick up, and hold, a high flying aircraft in the narrow beam.

Radar displays

To establish range from a radar set, a display called an 'A' scan was used. The radar 'picture' appeared as a horizontal line of green light across the width of the screen. Often there were two screens side by side, one a 'coarse' tube whose width represented the maximum range of the set, and the other a 'fine' tube, for accurate ranging. Conventionally, the left-hand edge of the line of animated 'grass' was zero range and the right-hand edge maximum range. Echoes, showing the presence of targets in the lobe, appeared as 'blips' on the trace and it was the shape of these echoes which were distinctively changed by the IFF transponder in a friendly aircraft. Superimposed on the trace was a brightened spot called the strobe which could be traversed by the operator's ranging handwheel and in 'strobing the echo' the range of the target was measured. The same drive was geared to electrical transmitters which fed the range information to repeaters, fire control predictors and so on. They thus received accurate and continuous ranges and also a measure of the rate at which the range was changing. This 'range-rate' helped to establish the target speed—a vital quantity in the complex mathematical formulae of the fire control prediction problem.

The other type of display was the Plan Position Indicator, or PPI, associated with the warning sets. A line of light, rotating like the spoke of a wheel, represented the radar beam, and echoes showed up as smudges of light as it passed through their bearing. The cathode ray tube was treated with a fluorescent substance which gave persistence to the echo after the line of light had passed through it. Whenever the radar beam passed through the bow of the ship the aerial triggered a separate line of light to give an indication of ship's head and, since the PPI had a compass ring around its circumference, it was possible to see one's own course. A second ring, which moved as the ship altered course, translated the compass bearing of a target to 'relative bearing' with respect to 'own ship'. In Fig **a** it can be seen that ship's course—as shown by the 'ship's head' mark—is 260 degrees; that 'Target Compass Bearing' is 330 degrees; and that the 'Relative Bearing' is 'Green, 70 degrees'. In Fig **b**, we have altered course to 300 degrees, the Target Compass Bearing has not altered, but the Relative Bearing ring has revolved in sympathy with the ship and the Relative Bearing of the target is now 'Green, 30 degrees'.

By this means the warning radar could indicate the bearing of targets to the weapon systems, whose directors would train to the appropriate Relative Bearing. Because the centre of the PPI represented 'own ship', it follows that the range of the echo could also be found. It was usual for the scale of the radar 'picture' to be adjustable so that the diameter might represent, say, 20, 10, or 5 miles. It goes without saying that land echoes appeared almost like a chart, making the display invaluable for 'Blind Pilotage' in confined waters. It was also an enormous aid to station-keeping in convoy at night.

Nowadays almost all ships, merchantmen and men-o'-war, have a 'navigation set' specially for this purpose, with its own 'cheese' aerial. Key channel-marking buoys have radar reflectors fitted to them and one can see a scale picture of a fairway on a PPI display. With so many aids to navigation, the spate of collisions and groundings in the English Channel in 1971 become all the more incomprehensible.

a

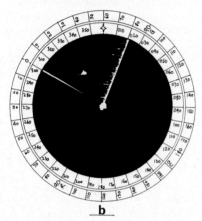

b

Above: *PPI presentation, described in text.*

Post-war naval radars

Type 960, another masthead dipole array, succeeded the earlier warning sets in large vessels and remained in service until fairly recently. With a need for even earlier warning in the missile age, very powerful sets indeed have been developed. Type 984 has an enormous single nacelle and was designed for aircraft carriers. Readers familiar with the Airfix *Victorious* will remember this vast unit. It is also carried by *Hermes* and *Eagle,* but is too large and heavy for smaller ships. Much more common is the 'bedstead' of Type 965, fitted in the 'Leanders', the 'Tribals' and the first of the Guided Missile Destroyers, as well as in *Blake.* The later Guided Missile Destroyers have a double-bedstead—as had the Air Direction 'Battles'—and *Ark Royal* has two.

A combined warning set called 993 is the successor to the original target indication 'cheeses' and most ships have this for gunnery direction. It has an odd-shaped aerial, but Type 974 and its variants—the 'navigation' sets—have retained the 'cheese' shape.

In general, British radar aerials have a neat appearance and in this respect contrast sharply with the large and clearly parabolic shapes common in the United States Navy and in continental ships. The design of some of the most modern aerials has reverted to the protective 'lantern' idea, in that they are contained within large mast-head spheres, often linked to complex computers and, not surprisingly, are referred to as 'crystal balls'!

Only a few of the older post-war frigates still retain Type 275 as a gunnery set; and with the passing of the battleship and cruiser the big DCT for their main armament has also disappeared—and with it Type 274. Only HMS *Belfast* remains so fitted.

All the old 'fishbone' arrays have vanished (although a few may be in service in ships sold abroad) and a new set called Type 262 has taken over from the close-range 'Yagi' aerials. This was first fitted in the STAAG twin Bofors and subsequently to the Close Range Blind Fire Director. The latest version of the latter is used to control certain 'Seacat' missile systems and the radar aerial is dish-shaped with full 'lock-on' facilities. Earlier applications of the CRBFD included the divided control of 'X' mounting in the 'Daring' class; the control of the twin 4 inch in the Type 15 frigates; and the control of twin and six-barrelled Bofors.

A less familiar radar was that linked to the American Mk 63 control system. This again had a dish-shaped aerial, but few were fitted in the RN. The complete set-up was fitted in *Victorious* where it controlled the USN 3 inch 50 calibre guns for which it had been originally designed, but it was also adapted for the British twin 4 inch and some of the 'Colony' class 6 inch cruisers were re-equipped with it during their final modernisation.

The standard gunnery radar in the British fleet today is known as Type 903. It has a large, fully stabilised dish on the right-hand side of its director, and mostly controls the modern 4.5 inch calibre gun, but also directs the 6 inch and 3 inch weapons in *Lion, Tiger* and *Blake.* A variant has been made for the latest 'Seacat' missile system.

A radar with a large nacelle, reminiscent of the 984 aerial in the carriers, is Type 901, the guidance radar for the Seaslug missile. Modellers of the Airfix *Devonshire* kit will remember that this overlooks the launcher on her quarterdeck. Another set found in the Guided Missile Destroyers is Type 278, a height finder, trunnioned like the old 277, which it closely resembles. There are other and bigger height finders in service but these are restricted in the main to aircraft carriers. They are easily recognisable because they are always mounted 'shaving-mirror' fashion.

One of the latest developments in weapon system control is the addition of a conventional television camera to the radar tracking head, providing a visual picture on special TV screens in the Operations Room below. A particularly ingenious arrangement has a 'search' radar, a 'tracker' radar and a TV camera in one unit. A conventional 'cheese' rotates constantly

A represents the basic form of the Type 79 and 279 series and B its successor, the Type 281. In both cases, the continuous wire-run starts at A and finishes at Z. The outside dimensions are correct for 1:600 scale, but can be considerably exceeded without appearing over-large. The smaller dipole aerials and the H/F D/F array can be made in the same way.

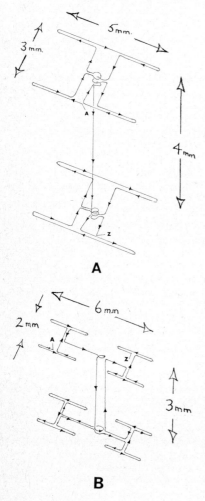

to provide a warning sweep; above, and co-axial with it, are the 'tracker' aerial and TV camera. When the warning radar detects a target, the tracker and TV lock on to it, while the lower aerial continues its uninterrupted sweep.

A possible drawback of this scheme is that the complicated unit cannot be protected by the spherical 'radome', unless it, too, rotates and has some kind of observatory-style shutters. However, sooner or later we will see a transparent sphere through which the TV camera can look; and when that arrives, there will be no prizes for guessing what its nickname will be. 'Crystal Ball, Mk II' perhaps?

Modelling the radar aerials

Accepting that the keen warship modeller has a fair degree of skill and patience, the level of accuracy he can achieve depends very largely on the size of the model. In the bigger scales—say 1:48—it is no more difficult to make a realistic aerial than it is to rig guardrails, but in the smaller models the task becomes increasingly difficult. Indeed, in 1:1200 it is virtually impossible, but this is far from being the case in the popular 1:600 scale of the Airfix kits.

In a number of these a useful selection of aerials is already available and most are easy to copy in scrap plastic. For the kit converter, who wishes to model, perhaps, *Suffolk* with her wartime fittings, the most likely area of difficulty will lie in making reasonable replicas of the dipole arrays of the early sets. For these fuse wire is by far the best medium provided one is prepared to compromise slightly on the exact dimensions.

Five amp wire is ideal and most households have a card containing enough for a whole model fleet somewhere near the fuse-box. The trick is to make the aerial from a continuous length of wire, doubling it back on itself where necessary. The sketches show the general idea.

Quite a good scheme is to push a needle into a flat piece of wood and 'build' the aerial around it. When complete, the aerial is slid off, dropped on to the mast and secured with a drop of cement. Choose a needle fractionally larger than the diameter of the mast and cement a tiny piece of scrap plastic to it in the appropriate position to prevent the aerial from slipping down: the scrap can always represent the drive motor.

Bending the fuse wire is best done with tweezers and their blade width forms a useful jig for dipole lengths.

Trying to produce aerials from extended plastic sprue is pretty well impossible, for although it is perfectly feasible to extend a sprue to hair thickness, the trouble is that it literally dissolves when an attempt is made to cement it. Further, unlike plastic, wire is malleable, so that, even if the final result is lop-sided, it can be eased to symmetry when in position.

The use of fuse wire can be extended to remake the 965 aerial provided as part 32 of the *Devonshire* kit. Here all one needs is a scrap of plastic of the same size as the kit part, around which the wire is wound in a continuous open coil. Leave enough 'tail' on the wire to run back to the mast, slide the coil carefully off the plastic jig, and an excellent 'open' aerial will result.

Wire can also be used to make the 'fish-bone' arrays. All they require is a tiny trough of paper, pierced with needle-point holes, through which twin 'sticks' are inserted. Make them plenty long enough and trim all at the same time with sharp scissors when their securing cement has set.

One final point about positioning aerials. The majority of modellers probably complete their ship kit in the full hull condition and in this case everything can be in the 'harbour stowed' position. If, however, the ship is worked into a dummy sea environment it is quite in order to set the aerials at random bearings (except, of course, the twin arrays of the early sets, mentioned above). For 'action' conditions, don't forget to train the appropriate director or DCT on to the same bearing as the armament. This is an error which many make, including maritime artists.

FIFTY YEARS OF THE IRISH AIR CORPS

By Gabriel T. Frost

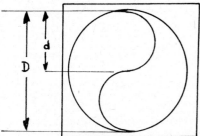

Above: *Celtic boss roundel type B. D=2d. Left hand portion green, right orange, white square used only when fuselage is of a dark colour. When placed on wings, the top of the roundel faces forward. No white square was used on wings.*

Below: *A number of Hawker Hurricanes strayed into Eire during 1942/3 and were interned. More of these aircraft were purchased from Britain after the war.*

The year 1972 saw the fiftieth anniversary of the founding of the Irish Air Corps, probably one of the least publicised anniversaries of the year. Despite Ireland's geographical proximity to Britain, the Air Corps of the Republic is almost unknown to the average British air enthusiast, yet it is a most interesting little force which has, over the years, been equipped with some useful aircraft—often for many years after they had gone out of service elsewhere. Irish air enthusiast Gabriel Frost here outlines the Air Corps history and suggests some simple models which can be made to depict several of its classic aircraft types.

OFFICIALLY, the Irish Air Corps was inaugurated when the National Army of the newly formed Irish Free State took over control of Baldonnel Aerodrome in February 1922. But before that, in 1921, a Martinsyde A Mk 2 was purchased to provide a quick getaway vehicle for General Michael Collins, Chief of Staff of the IRA (who had a price of £10,000 on his head), in the event of a breakdown of the delicate peace talks in which he was then engaged in London. In the event, however, all went well and the Martinsyde was flown to Ireland to become the first Air Corps aircraft in June 1922.

The first actual warplanes obtained by the Corps were Bristol Fighters, followed by Avro 504Ks and DH9s. Martinsyde F4s also saw service at this time. In 1926, the first new planes entered service, DH60 Moths, which were used as initial trainers. The 'Brisfits' and DH9s operated on policing and leaflet dropping missions, while the Martinsyde F4s and some of the DH9s, together with the DH60s and Avro 504Ks, were used for pilot training.

A Fairey IIIF was acquired in 1928 with float as well as normal wheel landing gear. It escorted the *Bremen* on its departure from Baldonnel at the start of its famous East-West crossing of the Atlantic. It later crashed into the garden of a house in Dublin. Vickers Vespas entered into service

Above: The model, and Below: The real thing—a Supermarine Spitfire T9 twin-seat trainer.

in 1930-31. One of them was later to crash while engaged in mock combat with the Cobham Air Circus. A number of Avro 621/626/631/636 type aircraft were obtained in the early 1930s and used as trainers until the 1940s. A De Havilland Dragon was also bought but finished its target tug career when it crashed with locked controls in 1941. Avro Ansons were purchased between 1937 and 1939 for coastal patrol duties, while Gloster Gladiators entered service in the fighter protection role.

Since Ireland was a neutral nation during World War 2, three Supermarine Walrus amphibians were acquired and operated on behalf of the Irish Naval Service on reconnaissance missions. Miles Magisters served as trainers during the war period and after. Delivery commenced in 1939 of a batch of Lysanders, which were found extremely suitable for operations from small fields during Army manoeuvres. They were later converted to target tugs and used as such until retirement in the late 1940s. Even though they were found unsuitable for use in their original roles, Hawker Hinds and Hectors were converted for use as trainers, a role they fulfilled until retirement in 1944.

A Lockheed Hudson, which landed by mistake in Sligo in 1941, was interned, as was a Fairey Battle target tug, which made a timely arrival since the Dragon, as previously recorded, was fated to crash a few months later. Some Hawker Hurricanes which strayed into Ireland in 1942-43 were also interned. Almost as if in retaliation for the internments, a Walrus was stolen from Shannon (Rineanna aerodrome) and later sighted by the British Coast Guard in Cornwall. A Whitley, which ditched in Galway Bay, sank before salvage could be initiated and a Sunderland of 201 Squadron RAF was lost in the Shannon estuary in a like manner. A Liberator and some Blenheims were damaged beyond repair in crash landings, as was an FW 200.

More Hawker Hurricanes were obtained after the war, while Miles Master trainers saw great service in training pilots during the later war years. Miles Martinet target tugs were purchased to replace the aging Lysanders in 1946. The last of the Martinets was not scrapped until 1963. One of the Avro XIX Ansons delivered in 1946 and used for transport duties was still in service in 1971 and was painted in RAF colours for film purposes in 1970. Supermarine Seafires were introduced into service in 1947 and were in existence until 1962 when the last of them was scrapped. The last of the Spitfire T9 trainers, which were delivered in 1951, was sold in 1968.

De Havilland Chipmunks entered service in 1952 and are still in use as initial trainers. De Havilland Doves are used for communications and NavAid calibration as well as aerial photography. Percival Provosts are used as advanced trainers, while five Vampire T55s are in front-line service. The most modern of Irish Air Corps equipment is the Alouette III, of which there are three in service. They are used for rescue work, which role they fulfill with distinction, along with that of aerial ambulance and Army liaison.

So, it may be said that the Irish Air Corps officers and men are able to run it smoothly and efficiently. It fulfills its purpose and serves its country as a section of the army faithfully, even though most of its efforts pass unnoticed in the eyes of the general public.

Above: The author's model of a Bristol Fighter, the first warplane to serve with the Irish Air Corps. Below: One of the De Havilland Chipmunks which are still in service.

Markings

(A) The earliest type of markings used by the Air Corps were green, white and orange stripes positioned chordwise slightly inboard on the top surfaces of the upper wings and on the lower surfaces of the bottom wings, on biplanes only. The orange was always outermost with white in the centre and green inside. A similar arrangement existed for the rudder, on which the stripes were vertical and with the orange on the right-hand side. Serial numbers were on the fuselage sides only, usually in black, just forward of the tailwings.

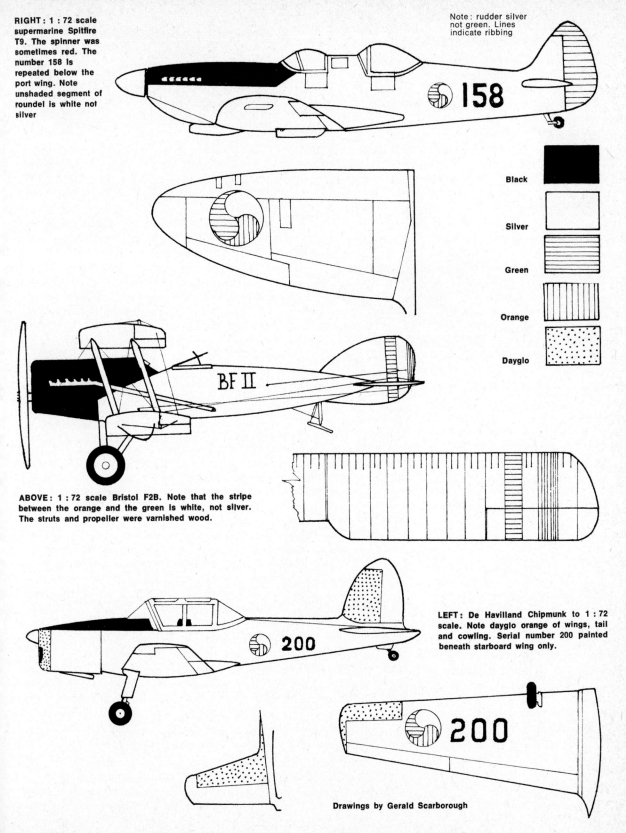

RIGHT: 1 : 72 scale supermarine Spitfire T9. The spinner was sometimes red. The number 158 is repeated below the port wing. Note unshaded segment of roundel is white not silver

Note: rudder silver not green. Lines indicate ribbing

Black

Silver

Green

Orange

Dayglo

ABOVE: 1 : 72 scale Bristol F2B. Note that the stripe between the orange and the green is white, not silver. The struts and propeller were varnished wood.

LEFT: De Havilland Chipmunk to 1 : 72 scale. Note dayglo orange of wings, tail and cowling. Serial number 200 painted beneath starboard wing only.

Drawings by Gerald Scarborough

Fifty Years of the Irish Air Corps

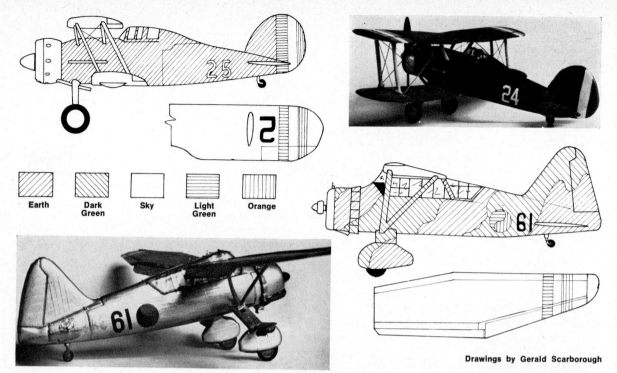

Earth | Dark Green | Sky | Light Green | Orange

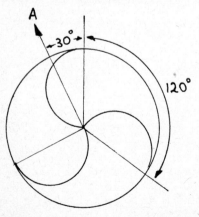

Drawings by Gerald Scarborough

Above: *Irish Air Corps Gloster Gladiator and Westland Lysander. Wing stripes and rudder markings on Gladiator are green/white/orange. The green and orange celtic boss is used on wing uppersurfaces instead of stripes. Gladiator engine cowling has bronze front and polished metal rear section. Gladiator fuselage numbers are white, all other numbers black. The Lysander model is shown in overall silver, while the drawing shows the earlier camouflage scheme.*

Below: *Celtic boss roundel type C. Segments reading clockwise from point A are white/orange/green. When positioned on fuselage sides, point A is vertical; on wings it must point forward.*

(B) This type superseded the above in 1938 and consisted of green, white and orange stripes below the wings as described in (A). A two-colour celtic boss (orange and green) was worn on the wing upper-surfaces and on the fuselage sides, sometimes in a white square (when positioned on a dark background). On the roundel, the orange was always on the right.

(C) Introduced in 1952, this set of markings consisted of a tricoloured celtic boss, which was carried in the six standard positions. The colours used are green, white and orange, which were positioned as in the drawing. Black numerals worn on fuselage sides and below the right-hand wing.

Models

The following descriptions relate to the 17 subjects in the Airfix range which can be converted to represent Air Corps aircraft. In most cases, the only converting necessary is in the markings and colour schemes. References to *Airfix Magazine* conversion articles, where appropriate, are included. In each case the serials come first, followed by the delivery dates, with colour schemes, markings and other necessary data on the subject.

(1) **Avro 504K:** A1 to A6. Delivered in mid-1922. Silver overall with natural polished wood struts, propeller, etc. Marking scheme (A). Possibly Roman numerals used. Use basic Airfix kit suitably painted.

(2) **Bristol F2B:** BF1 to BF8, 17 to 22. Delivered 1922-25. Silver fuselage/wings, with black nose cowling, except BF7 which had dark green upper-surfaces and natural fabric under-surfaces, with black nose. Marking scheme (A). BF series had Roman numerals high on fuselage sides behind gunner's cockpit in black except BF7 which had white numbers. The other (17 to 22) series used black numbers positioned as on Avro 504K in ordinary style. Use basic Airfix kit.

(3) **De Havilland DH9:** Nos 1 to 8. Delivered 1923-29. Silver fuselage and wings with battleship grey front cowling and rear fuselage under tailwings. Marking scheme (A). Roman numerals on fuselage sides in black ahead of tailwings. Convert Airfix DH4 as per *Airfix Magazine* February 1968.

Above, *top to bottom: Irish Air Corps Vickers Vespa, Miles Magisters and Avro XIX Anson; author's models of IAC Avro 504K, Hawker Hind and Miles Master.* **Below right:** *IAC Supermarine Walrus.*

(4) **Avro Anson Mk I:** A19 to A22, 41 to 45. Delivered 1937-39. Earth upper-surfaces and black under-surfaces or standard camouflage with black undersurfaces. First planes to use marking scheme (**B**). Black numerals. Use basic Airfix kit.

(5) **Gloster Gladiator:** 23 to 26. Delivered 1938. Earth upper fuselage and wing top surfaces. Sky or light grey under-surfaces, wheel hubs and undercarriage legs. Marking scheme (A). White numerals on fuselage sides, black under wings. Use basic Airfix kit, suitably painted.

(6) **Supermarine Walrus:** Nos 18 to 20. Delivered 1939. Earth overall at first, then silver overall. Marking scheme (A). Use basic Airfix kit.

(7) **Westland Lysander:** Nos 61 to 66. Delivered 1939. Standard earth/green camouflage at first, with black under-surfaces. Later, earth upper-surfaces and Sky under-surfaces. When converted to target tugs, they were silver overall. Marking scheme (B) with black numerals on fuselage sides behind celtic boss. Use basic Airfix kit.

(8) **Hawker Hind/Hector:** Hind: 67 to 72. Delivered 1940. Hector: 78 to 90, delivered 1941-42. Silver overall, with marking scheme (B). For Hind, modify Airfix Demon, for Hector convert Airfix Demon or Hart as per *Airfix Magazine* June, 1965.

(9) **Lockheed Hudson:** No 91 interned 1941. Standard earth/green upper-surfaces with black under-surfaces. Possibly earth overall later. Marking scheme (B) with fuselage roundel in white square. Use basic Airfix kit.

(10) **Fairey Battle:** No 92 interned 1941. Standard target tug finish when first acquired, later earth or silver overall. Marking scheme (B) with black numerals. Use basic Airfix kit.

(11) **Hawker Hurricane:** Nos 93 to 95 interned 1942-43. Nos 103 to 112 delivered 1943-44. Nos 114 to 120 delivered 1945. Grey/green camouflage upper-surfaces with light grey under-surfaces. Marking scheme (B) with fuselage roundel in white square. Black numerals. Use basic Airfix kit.

(12) **Avro XIX Anson:** Nos 141 to 143. Delivered 1946. Silver overall with matt black anti-dazzle panel on nose. Marking scheme (**B**) with addition of small Irish flag on tail fin. Convert Airfix Mk I as per *Airfix Magazine*, February 1971.

(13) **Supermarine Seafire LF3:** Nos 146 to 157. Delivered 1947. Matt green overall. Marking scheme (B) with roundel on white square on fuselage sides. Modify Airfix kit.

(14) **Supermarine Spitfire T9:** Nos 158 to 163. Delivered 1951. Green overall at first, then silver overall with black cowling top. Marking scheme (B) at first, then scheme (C). Convert Airfix Mk 9 as per *Airfix Magazine*, September 1966.

(15) **De Havilland Chipmunk:** Nos 164 to 175. Delivered 1952, 199/200 delivered 1965. Silver overall with dayglo nose panels, wingtips, fin and tailplanes. Marking scheme (C). Use basic Airfix kit.

(16) **DH Dove:** Nos 176, 188, 194, 201/EI-ARV. Delivered 1952/59/62/71. Silver overall with dayglo nose, tail, wingtips and elevators. Marking scheme (C). Convert Airfix Heron as per *Airfix Magazine*, December 1966.

Percival Provost: Nos 177 to 184 Mk 51. Delivered 1954/55. Nos 189-190, Mk 53, delivered 1960. Silver basic with dayglo propeller spinner, wingtips, tailfin and tailplanes. Marking scheme (C) with black numerals on fuselage sides and below wing. Convert Airfix Jet Provost.

THE PICK OF PHOTOPAGE

From *AIRFIX* magazine files

Above: *Spitfire Mk Vb of 457 Squadron RAAF, BP-E, AB138, at Andreas, Isle of Man, February 1942 (Frank S. Smith).* **Above right:** *Handley Page 1500, circa 1917. Note folding wings to enable the aircraft to fit into its hangar, and the early Clayton caterpillar tractor (Group Captain W. S. O. Randle).* **Right:** *Meteor FR9 of No 2 Squadron, Gutersloh, Germany, being refuelled (G. P. Young). This photograph suggests diorama possibilities utilising a converted Airfix Scammel truck and Meteor.* **Below right:** *Covenanter 15-ton bridgelayer with scissors-type bridge. This was one of the vehicles supplied to the Australian Army in 1944, and used operationally in SE Asia and the SW Pacific area. This example is still preserved in Australia (Allen Seymour).*

Top right: *Czechoslovak Avia 534. Note the tail raised on an oil drum as a trestle, probably for maintenance purposes* (C. Imull). **Above right:** *Naval 12 pdrs taken from HMS* Juno, *in action near Basreh in the Persian Gulf in 1916. Note the Lee Enfield rifles stacked on the left, and the bandolier containing 120 rounds of ammunition worn by each man* (Len Mainwaring). **Right:** *C-141A-LM Starlifter No 40650 of 60 Military Airlift Wing at Travis AFB, California, in 1971. Note two badges on tail—60 MAWg and 938 MA Group* (Peter N. Simpson). **Below right:** *Canadian Harvard II. Note bomb racks beneath wing* (M. J. Stephens). **Bottom row, l-r:** *Covenanter of the Polish 10th Mounted Rifles Regiment in France after D-Day. Note especially the unit markings* (J. Kaye); *Type 14 mobile radar (ground control interception) mounted on Austin K6 chassis* (Ray Stanton); *and Mk IIA medium tank: obsolete by the time of World War 2, a number of these vehicles were nevertheless dug-in as fixed gun emplacements at Mersa Matruh in 1940.* (R. T. C. Prentice).

The Pick of Photopage

Above: *Two De Havilland Tiger Moths in Finland in the 1930s. The aircraft in the foreground has the name* Ilmatar *painted on the engine cowling, the one in the background was called* Lokki *(Esa Savola). The serial OH-ILA is repeated across the top wing. Provost T1 of the Irish Air Corps. The serial number beneath the 'C'-type celtic boss (see Fifty Years of the Irish Air Corps) appears to be 24 VOCT 6 (Donald Stirling).* **Right,** *top to bottom: German airmen about to moor the airship* Graf Zeppelin *to a portable mooring mast, August 1937 (C. S. Lockwood). DH 10, serial number F1874, at Martlesham Heath in 1919-20 (Group Captain W. S. O. Randle). The Polish destroyer* Lightning *during World War 2. Note positioning of the AA armament and torpedo tubes. The ship is flying a White Ensign from her topmast and the Polish national flag from her stern (N. Wrobel). French AMX 13 light tanks moving through Port Said at the time of the Anglo-French invasion of the Suez Canal Zone in 1956 (M. K. Brown). Colour was sand overall with a dark blue stripe around the turret. The serial number on the vehicle in the centre is B31491.*

Right: *Martin Marlin flying boat of the US Navy during a visit to Singapore in 1958. The serial number is VP 46, and the crew's names appear to be stencilled beneath the cockpit* (D. M. Stanley). *Armstrong-Whitworth Siskins of 29 and 56 Squadrons at Hendon Air Display 1929* (Group Captain W. S. O. Randle). *Lancaster B1(FE) of No 7 Squadron, serial TW659, at Changi, Singapore, in early 1947* (Peter Finch). *Colour scheme is white upper-surface and black undersurface. Lockheed P-38 Lightning at Selkirk, date unknown. Note US flag on nose* (Donald Stirling). **Below:** *Bofors 40 mm anti-aircraft gun at the School of Artillery, Palestine, during the early 1940s* (J. Bramfitt). *Note the white-walled tyres. Valentine tank with canvas 'lorry' camouflage loaded on a Scammel tank transporter, Western Desert 1942* (S. C. Millar). *American 'Honey' reconnaissance tank with turret removed, in service with the Polish 10th Mounted Rifles Regiment in France, 1944* (J. Kaye). **Bottom right:** *A British 3-inch and a German 81 mm mortar* (K. Bryers). *Note the different-shaped ammunition containers. The German crewmen are wearing early-pattern tunics with bottle green collars. Note the gas mask container slung on the front of the belt of the German soldier on the right, instead of its usual place on the back. The British soldier on the right is holding the mortar's leather muzzle cap.*

The Pick of Photopage

NARROW GAUGE SADDLE TANK

By Les Andrews

One of the best known of model narrow gauge layouts is the Ambledown Railway, built by Les Andrews. It depicts a typical British narrow gauge line in the style of those that flourished in real life in the earlier part of this century. Les Andrews has given the line a lot of charm and individuality by converting and adapting from ordinary kits. One of his latest models is a neat combination of the Airfix 'Pug' saddle tank with a Minitrains chassis. The result is most appealing and an ideal model for anyone wishing to get started with a small narrow gauge layout. Michael Andress took the pictures when visiting the Ambledown Railway, and Les Andrews tells how he made the model.

AS SOON AS I saw the Airfix LYR 'Pug' Saddle Tank in 00 scale on the shelves of my model shop, my mind turned to the possibility of using this kit for the basic body on a narrow gauge locomotive in 009 gauge using the readily available Minitrains Baldwin 0-4-0T chassis. After purchasing both the Airfix kit and a Minitrains chassis I soon found that my hopes had been justified and that a quite passable conversion was possible with a little cutting and juggling of the very good mouldings in the kit.

The cab sides in the kit are much too long for our purpose and need to be cut. Using a sharp craft knife and a steel straight edge, remove ¼ inch out of each cab side moulding in such a way as to leave the entrance and side rails intact. Then re-join the edges. Also remove the steps up to the cab, as these reach too far down for narrow gauge locomotives. Replace these with smaller steps constructed of black plastic card. The roof needs a similar ¼ inch reduction, and the front of the cab must be cut just inside

Below: *The model with the moulded handrails as in the original kit shown at Ambledown station. The loco has a neat appearance but looks even better, as can be seen in the pictures on the following pages, if these handrails are replaced with separate ones made from nickel silver wire.*

Right: *The locomotive seen in rural surroundings on the Ambledown Railway, the two coaches it is pulling have bodies scratch built from plastic card. The sky effect in the background is achieved by placing an illustration of some clouds behind the baseboard. When photographed from a low level it results in a very realistic 'sky'.*

the line of rivets which show under the spectacles on the boiler side, so that this front will just clear the motor of the chassis over which it rests when made up into the complete cab.

The whole four sides of the cab and roof may now be glued or 'welded' together. (I prefer the welding method using Slater's excellent Mekpak fluid with a fine brush. This enables you to put the stuff just where it is required and not all over the mouldings, to their subsequent detriment.) It will be found that with a slight amount of juggling this cab will set firmly upon the chassis and may, in fact, be aligned and fixed to the chassis body members.

To clear the motor and mechanism it is necessary to cut down the two boiler sides. If this cut is made just into the right angle at the bottom of the saddle tanks where they join the representation of the springs, it will be found that when mated with the smoke box door section the whole boiler assembly can be fixed both to the cab, and at the front to the bar holding the front coupling pin of the chassis. As the front join is only a light one it can be undone using a sharp knife blade to expose the mechanism for any servicing it requires, from time to time, although I have found that these little mechanisms run for considerable periods with the minimum of attention.

You have now constructed the basic locomotive and even in this raw state I think it has quite a pleasing appearance. This can be very much enhanced, however, with a little thought. Name and number plates, wire insets in the spectacle holes and a driver perhaps.

In addition to the above I have, as an experiment, replaced the moulded plastic rails along the tank sides with Messrs K's handrail knobs and nickel silver wire sold in model railway shops), a fiddling job perhaps, but I rather like the effect. Removal of the moulding is quite simple with a sharp craft knife, taking care to watch both any surrounding detail and the fingers! Without this last refinement, however, I still think that the original moulding is quite satisfactory and the finished locomotive will be a further variant in your stud.

A final word. You will end up with a lot of bits of the kit left over and these can be put in your scrapbox. You end up with a little narrow gauge locomotive of character, freelance it is true, but very typical of its type.

Below, left to right: *Loco seen from the front with new nickel silver railings added to the sides and front; bodywork removed to show engine detail taken from a Minitrains chassis; rear view of model with engine just visible in the cab doorway. All paint on this model is black Floquil, although other types of paint could be used to achieve the same effect.*

Narrow Gauge Saddle Tank

ARMIES BY THE DOZEN

By D. V. Oakley

Above from top to bottom: *Confederate infantry painted up straight from the Airfix set; Union Iron Brigade from the same set, only modification is painting detail and the addition of a small blanket roll to the top of the pack; Sardinian Bersaglieri with altered hats to tilt down at right and a falling cock's plume made from Plasticine; German Colonial Troops with hat brim turned up at right and musket repainted to look like a German Mauser rifle. All these different troops have been made from the Airfix Confederate infantry set entailing at the most some Plasticine additions and different painting detail. The basic figures remain unaltered.*

THERE ARE THOSE of us who, with infinite and painstaking care, sit, lens to eye, painting the hobnails on an 00/HO soldier's raised boot. Others send their armies into battle equipped only with a rudimentary blob of pink for face and hands. Still others decide that nothing but an army of 500 bashi-bazooks converted from the Robin Hood set will satisfy their Napoleonic urge. This article is for those who are, like me, dissatisfied with leaving things alone, but too lazy or impatient to devote the time and energy needed for a top-class conversion job.

I have often been asked, 'What can I do with my Confederates?' Biting back the immediate and obvious answer, I ask what's wrong with them. I'm usually told that the trouble lies with the hat. 'A little knowledge is a dangerous thing', and my questioners, having done some research, have found that the Confederates wore kepis. Therefore they have scrapped their Confederates and begun painting Union men grey. Their problem is, what to do with a superannuated, inaccurate army—a problem also confronting the rulers of certain impoverished republics.

The first thing to realise is that whatever the planners or officers said, the men on both sides discarded at the first opportunity those articles of clothing which were uncomfortable or inconvenient to wear. Both sides used each other's discarded equipment when their own ran short (for example, after First Bull Run the Confederates were glad to 'acquire' bits of Union equipment ranging from water-bottles to cannon), and both sides plonked hats of unorthodox design at rakish angles upon their heads. This was no 'spit and polish' European war, but one in which armies were either amateur and enthusiastic, or conscripted and rebellious. There was no regimental tradition in the accepted European sense.

When this is realised, and when you also realise that 'the Blue and the Grey' really meant 'the Blue and the Off-white, Darkish-brown, Yellowish-khaki, Butternut or Greenish' you have the first inkling of how to handle your Confederates. You can paint them all sorts of colours and still claim authenticity.

The 'regular' Confederate army can certainly be given slouch hats of varying shades of grey, brown or black. Their appearance can be improved by the addition of a blanket roll (made of Plasticine) slung diagonally shoulder to waist on those figures that will take it, and trousers can be carved down at the ankles to provide a 'tied-in' effect. It is probably more effective, if less authentic, to give your entire army uniform coats—either Butternut (yellow-brown) or grey—and to achieve the ragged effect by varying the colours of the trousers, hat, equipment straps, etc. The Confederate army in the last year of the war was in a parlous state of *déshabillé*—resulting from lack of sufficient supplies, due to the Union blockade of the South.

Doubtless some people would like a more uniform force. I would suggest that the Union Iron Brigade, wearing black slouch hats, dark blue coats and light blue 'Government' trousers, might meet the case here. Purists will probably object to the length of the coat, but if it is a case of 'the game's the thing' and you can tell what they're meant to be, I shouldn't worry too much. You can do a lot to make up for deficiencies in the original figure by precise painting of what *is* there, and by slight alteration. If you find, after research, that you need a slouch hat that turns up on the left, just slice off the Airfix hat with a razor blade and glue it on again back to front!

Below top: *Boer commandos suitable for use any time between the Great Trek of 1830 and the Boer War of 1899; Spanish Colonial infantry dressed in white duck uniforms with black webbing and rifles provided from the World War 1 British infantry set.*

Above bottom: *South American insurgents converted from Confederate infantry with the skilful use of Plasticine and paint. Note also the rather floppy sombreros achieved by replacing the original hat brim by one made from plastic card or stiff paper; Naval landing party that can represent either Royal Navy or Imperial Russian Navy sailors as they both wore the same type of dress and equipment.*

It may be that your tastes run to more unusual and even exotic troops. I have often thought that the patchwork of small states that made up Italy before unification might provide a fertile ground for imaginative wargaming, and you could do worse than to start your Italian armies with a regiment of Sardinian Bersaglieri (1860).

These troops wore dark blue uniforms with collars, pointed cuffs and epaulettes in scarlet and a scarlet trouser seam. Coats were double-breasted with aiguillettes of rifle-green. They were a crack light infantry regiment, as indeed are their modern descendants.

Bersaglieri were characterised by broad-brimmed, black hats with round crowns, worn dashingly tilted to the right, and decorated with a somewhat Ruritanian cascade of cock's feather, also at the right. You can make this plume from a heavily scored blob of Plasticine or a simple cut-out from paper.

Bersaglieri battalions fought with distinction against Naples in 1860, and their uniform remained basically the same until World War 1, so you could also use them in small Colonial-style wars. (They were, apparently, part of the Italian contingent sent to the relief of the Legations at Peking during the Boxer Rebellion.) The running Confederate infantryman is an ideal subject for conversion if you have the patience to carve down his legs to make ankle-length gaiters and tilt his hat to the required angle.

The last years of the nineteenth century saw the European empires at the height of their power. This includes Imperial Germany, who, determined upon finding her place in the sun, annexed 'German South West Africa'. In Africa the German troops wore a smart light grey uniform with brown leather jackboots and equipment, and a grey slouch hat. The collar and cuffs were blue, as was the pagri (wide hat band) and the piping down the opening of the single-breasted jacket. The hat was turned up at the right, and had the Imperial German red/white/black roundel apparently covering the pin used to hold the turn-up in place. The Confederate infantryman at the advance is the figure to use as a basis here. If you are absolutely set on authenticity the musket must be removed and replaced by one from the World War 1 German infantry set.

The British, too, had their troubles in South Africa, fighting two fierce wars against the Boers. The first Boer War ended in the ignominious defeat of the British at Majuba Hill in the 1880s, when a British column fell into a Boer ambush and was shot to pieces by an enemy who was adept at taking cover, used to firearms since childhood, superb at fieldcraft, and convinced that he represented the wrath of God against the hosts of Midian.

The Boers lived by farming and hunting, and raised their 'commandos' on an *ad hoc* basis, with 'every man his own general'. They wore no uniform, but were characterised by broad-brimmed hats, often turned up at the side or in front, and most of them wore bristling patriarchal beards. In fact, they looked remarkably like the Airfix Confederates, and if you paint them in dark brown, green, grey, black, navy blue and similar sober colours you will have a force of Boers that will do duty for any period between the Great Trek (1830) and the second Boer War (1899-1902). The only other adjustment needed is to replace the existing muskets with those of the World War 1 Germans.

Incidentally, it was during the Great Trek period that the Zulus first felt the effect of massed musketry and cannon, suffering a crushing defeat at the hands of the Boers at Blood River. Despite suicidal bravery the Zulus were unable to get near the Boer laager, and the Boer victory, leading to the foundation of the Orange Free State and the Transvaal, has led to the keeping of the anniversary as a public holiday in South Africa to this day.

Winston Churchill, I believe, called the war between the United States and Spain, which broke out in 1898, 'A splendid little war'. The Spaniards, hampered by a prevailing Colonial lassitude typified by the word 'mañana' (tomorrow, or do tomorrow what can be done today), took the field in uniforms suspiciously like pyjamas, and despite isolated acts of heroism,

Above from top to bottom: *Basic unpainted figures in the centre with conversions either side showing that all you need to obtain a large and varied amount of troops is a steady hand, imagination and a good reference source; South American insurgent and original figure show the detail adjustment needed to make this rather unusual 'soldier'; Bersaglieri made from the Confederate running infantryman, shown alongside for comparison with the finished product.*

Below: *When painting figures of this small size it is advisable to carry out all the main undercoating while the figures are still on the sprue. For smaller detail work individual figures can be mounted on a pin, both these methods allow paint to dry without smudging and ensures that plastic and paper additions glued to the figures have a chance to set without being disturbed by clumsy fingers.*

such as the defence of El Caney, were soundly beaten and lost Cuba and the Phillipines to the USA.

The pyjama-like uniform referred to above was in fact of light white duck with narrow blue-grey stripes and red shoulder straps and cuffs. On his head the Spanish soldier wore a straw hat (natural colour) and his equipment was of black leather. A straight repaint job on the Airfix Confederate troops should do the trick here.

Whilst in Latin America, some mention must be made of the long record of civil disturbances in that unhappy hemisphere. I can't keep track of them all, but revolutionary armies from 1880 to the present day seem notable for their lack of military garb, and their motley collection of equipment.

If you want a fine, all-purpose set of banditos to foment trouble in your little 20 mm world, the Airfix Confederates are your men! Paint them white all over, then give them swarthy countenances and drooping mustachioes and, having removed all packs and straps, add gay sashes or Indian blankets draped over one shoulder, made from Plasticine. Remember, also, that you will have to carve down their boots to make passable sandals or swop their legs for those in the Indian set, building up body putty on the legs to make trousers.

Headgear can be a simple painting job on the existing hat, or you can remove the hat brim, cut a circle in plastic (or even paper at a pinch), punch out the middle and place the disc over the existing hat crown to make a very Mexican sombrero; then fix with Copydex adhesive. Thus equipped, your Revolutionaries can be set to fighting your Spaniards in tropical uniform, or even each other.

Whilst we're on the subject of Colonial wars and straw hats, Naval landing-parties are a reasonable addition to the well-equipped wargamer's forces, and, what is more, there is no need to worry about trying to disguise the Confederates' beards. Trim off the coat below the belt, and you have a very effective blouse top. Paint on the sailor's collar in blue, not forgetting the three white lines, though one will do if you have difficulty with this, and paint the rest of the uniform white, blue, blue over white, or white over blue. This is perfectly permissible because the Royal Navy had no overall dress regulations before 1857. Your sailors will look very effective in action against Boers, Fuzzy-Wuzzies, Zulus and assorted savages—perhaps the Airfix Arabs. The Navy was always trying to catch Arab slavers up the East African coast.

A word or two in conclusion. It strikes me that the dedicated modeller will be aware of the techniques to be used in basic conversion, and will probably object to the admitted approximation of the figures described above. The beginner, however, may not have thought of some of these ideas, and may well say, 'It's all very well saying what we can do, but you don't tell us *how*'.

The first essential is a good reference book. I have based much of this article on information culled from Rene North's *Military Uniforms, 1686-1918* available in paperback, and Kannick's *Military Uniforms of the World in Colour*. Another useful book for American Civil War uniforms is *American Civil War Infantry* by Michael Blake. The second essential is experience, and I have used what little I have for the rest of the article. A good, sharp modelling knife makes life much easier, if more bloodstained at the finger-ends, and I should use at least three types of glue—one epoxy resin, for permanence; one rubber-based like Copydex, for attaching small items; and one plastic cement for strictly temporary joins. Matt paint is generally considered best for cloth, and gloss for leather, but this is very much a matter of preference—gloss is held to be harder wearing. Always use the best brush you can afford, and clean it carefully after use. Some people use a magnifying lens for detailed work. Finally, don't be discouraged. Even your worst work will be better than leaving your army in its box, because it will be *your* work, your very own, and a little bit of you will have gone into it.

SOLDIER	HAT AND COAT	TROUSERS AND BOOTS	PACK AND WEBBING	RIFLE	TRIMMING	NOTES
CONFEDERATE	Hat: As existing. Nos 26, 27, 29, 34 and HM4. Coat: Butternut, No 26 lightened with 7 and 34	Trousers: Officially light blue but in practice any sober colour. Boots: Black or brown, sometimes none worn	Pack: Officially blacked but often of indeterminate colour. Webbing: Colour as above	As existing. Finish silver for Government issue or brown for non-standard equipment	Blue at cuff, not always worn	Paint face flesh with a touch of brick red and tan. Add beard if desired. A blanket roll was worn diagonally across the shoulder. Bore hole between arm and torso to take this. Officers' coats can be painted with No 27, if gloves are to be worn paint with Nos 7 or 9
UNION IRON BRIGADE	Hat: As existing, No M33. Coat: Dark blue, No 15+ black matted, or military Dark Blue	Trousers: Light blue, No 48 matted. Boots: Black gloss overlaid with streaks of white paint to simulate dust	Pack: Gloss black canvas frame. Trim off blanket roll and replace with roll of plasticine. Webbing: Gloss black, No 21, haversack carried on left hip, white on white strap	As above	None. Officers' epaulettes blue with gold bars	Face as above. Small blanket roll worn on top of pack, blue or grey with white strap. Officers' gloves: Nos 7 or 9
SAILOR	Hat: As existing but can be repositioned, No 7 matted with matting agent. Trim off below waist leaving ammunition pouches. Paint navy or white	Trousers: White or blue. Boots: Black	Pack: Not worn. Webbing: White No 34 on blue. Blouses, pale blue on white	As above with browned barrel	Square at back painted light blue outlined in white	Face as above. Outline straps etc, in grey or black to make them stand out
GERMAN COLONIAL	Hat: As existing turned up at right, No 27 with 34. Coat: Light grey, No 27 with 34	Trousers: As coat, blue stripe, worn tucked into jackboots. Boots: Tan No 9	Pack: None. Webbing: Tan No 9. Straps of the vertical 'braces' type. Probably crossed at back	As above, or replace with rifle from World War 1 German set. Colour black barrel, brown wood	Blue collar, cuffs and line down front, No 48 matted. Bars of red outlined white on collar and cuffs	Cockade on right side of hat is red, white, black, reading from the centre. Hats trimmed in blue
BERSAGLIERI	Hat: As existing but repositioned to tilt well down at right. No 33, plume various shades of green. Coat: Dark blue as Union Iron Brigade	Trousers: As coat, scarlet side seam, PLAKA 24. Boots: Black, ankle-length	Pack: None. Webbing: Black, ammunition pouches carried centrally on the waist belt	As existing	Collar and cuffs red, PLAKA 24. Aiguillettes, PLAKA emerald 43	Falling plume of cock's feathers at right reading from plasticine. Paint faces as above with small pointed beards. Black leather gloves worn, No 27
BOER	Hat: As existing in dark colours or various shades of brown. Coat: Any sober shade, eg. dark brown, black etc	Trousers: Of any sober shade matching or contrasting with coat. Boots: Black or brown, often knee length	Pack: If the original figure wears one it can be retained painted in any dark colour. Webbing: Frequently of brown leather, could also be captured British bandolier equipment in khaki or white	As existing for Great Trek replace with rifle from World War 1 German set for Boer War	None	Paint face as usual but add large beards. Blankets worn as for Confederates. Hats were of civilian manufacture as was the dress in general. Only belts and packs were of a military nature, if worn at all
SPANISH COLONIAL (TROPICAL)	Hat: As existing, No 7 with matting agent. Coat: White, No 34 with stripes of pale blue, No 47 matted	Trousers: As coat with red side seam, but see 'Note' at right. Boots: Black	Pack: Brown No 29. Webbing: Black	As existing but can be replaced with rifles from World War 1 British or German sets	Red shoulder straps and cuffs	Paint faces as before, aim at a swarthy complexion with a small moustache. Coat distinctions are of regimental facing colour. Retain rolled greatcoat, colour No 27
SOUTH AMERICAN INSURGENT	Hat: Remove brim and replace with plastic card disc, No 7 and 26 or 28. Coat: Not worn, trim down for shirt effect, remove pack, etc, paint No 34	Trousers: Same colour as shirt. Boots: Not worn, paint white to represent sandals or bare feet	Pack: Not worn. Webbing: Seldom in evidence, if worn, paint white to match or tone with clothing	As existing. Finish in dirty colours or bright silver	None	Sash painted on or poncho or blanket draped over shoulder made from plasticine Paint all these to simulate folded Indian work. Try for a motley appearance as no guerilla looked quite the same as any of his comrades

Note: Numbers in table above refer to Humbrol paint coding which can be found in any Humbrol catalogue. If PLAKA poster colours are used, a matt white undercoat is needed and a clear varnish on completion as extra protection. I would suggest that you coat any figures with Unibond adhesive as this gives a firm base for paints and ensures that they do not flake with handling.

It is perfectly possible to give these figures faces, and a remarkable improvement in these can be achieved by using white for the eyes with a spot of brown or green for the pupil. Black or blue tends to give the figure a disconcertingly aggressive and somewhat lunatic stare!

Armies by the Dozen

THE LOCKHEED HUDSON

By Michael J. F. Bowyer

'HUDSONS of Coastal Command last night attacked enemy shipping off the Dutch coast. Hits were scored on a 2,000-ton coaster. From these operations, two of our aircraft are missing.' Familiar, indeed, were such words in 1941 and 1942, when squadrons of Coastal Command maintained a significant offensive against enemy coastal traffic. Hudsons searched extensively for enemy warships and submarines, finding similar employment with American and Commonwealth Air Forces. Their ancestry made them ideal transport aircraft in the Middle and Far East. Thus, the wheel of development completed one involved turn.

Quite a furore was created when, in June 1938, Air Ministry purchased 200 Lockheed 14 bombers to be used as navigation trainers. This, and the announcement that the RAF was also to use Harvard trainers, produced the inevitable outcry among those ever-ready to sell British aircraft abroad, but less eager for reciprocal trade. Events proved the wisdom of the decision, for the Lockheed aircraft neatly filled a gap in Coastal Command's equipment. As war clouds gathered, the Command was using an array of biplane flying-boats and short-range Ansons. The Botha was not progressing well and the Beaufort lagging behind, so it was decided to employ Hudsons as general reconnaissance bombers.

The Lockheed 14 was an enlarged, improved design stemming from the Lockheed 10 and 12 transports, and made its first flight on July 29 1937. N7205, the first Hudson, flew on December 10 1938. It had more powerful engines than the Lockheed 14, a clear nose, two forward-firing machine guns and provision for a bulbous turret aft of the entry door. On February 15 1939 the first Hudson was unloaded at Liverpool Docks and taken to Speke for assembly, where many others were to follow before air delivery commenced during November 1940.

Right: *Hudson serial number T9303 just after take-off from its base at Bircham Newton, Norfolk, in September 1940.* **Below:** *Inside the cockpit of the same aircraft. The pilot has his hands on the engine throttle controls and the passage way to the right gives access to the nose compartment for the bomb aimer and observation positions.*

Above: *Another view of Hudson T9303. The colour scheme was dark green/dark earth/night. Note the wavy line finish. The yellow outer of the fuselage roundel is clearly a later addition to the original roundel, typical of the 1940 period. The paintwork of both the roundel outer and the code letter are carried over the fuselage transparency.*

Over 2,000 Hudsons were built, but not all of those produced or earmarked for Britain reached the RAF. Many were diverted to the RAAF, RCAF, RNZAF and the United States forces. British orders for the Hudson I totalled 350 aircraft: N7205-7404, P5116-5165 and T9266-9365. The remainder of the last batch were delivered as Mk IIs, serials T9366-9385, which could be distinguished from earlier aircraft by their spinner-less Hamilton Standard Hydromatic airscrews. Such propellers are supplied with the Airfix model of this aircraft. The N-serialled aircraft at first wore dark green and dark earth upper surfaces, and had black under-surfaces whereon the serial appeared in white in the customary pre-war bomber styling. Roundels were in keeping with the styles of the period. Early in 1940 these Hudsons in many cases adopted silver undersurfaces, retained until the summer of 1940 when they were changed to Sky. Code letters remained medium grey, although some squadrons carried very light grey codes. Although none of those which I saw had Sky codes, it seems feasible that some of the Hudsons carried them.

The brown-green Sky finish was retained until 1943, when the Hudsons, then mainly employed on anti-submarine duty, came more into line with the flying-boats, and had white sides and undersurfaces with the sickly slate green and grey upper decks. In such cases the code letters were black or dark grey like the fuselage serials. Overseas, the reconnaissance Hudsons bore similar colours and, when necessary, had SEAC roundels. Aircraft used by the RAAF in the disastrous campaign in Malaya in 1942 had the brown-green-black finish. Hudson transports of the Middle East squadrons wearing desert camouflage had red code letters. The camouflage consisted of two tones of brown on the upper surfaces and a rich and somewhat sickly azure blue on the undersurfaces.

Hudson IIIs, first delivered in the autumn of 1940, came into widespread use in 1941. They had 1,200 hp Cyclone GR-1820-G205A engines, and provisions for two beam guns and a ventral gun. The first batches were T9386-9465, V8975-8999 and V9020-9065. AM930-953 were also IIIs used mainly in the Far East. Additional tankage was provided in the other IIIs —V9066-9069, V9090-9129, 9150-9199, 9220-9254—many of which were supplied to the RCAF and RNZAF. To distinguish the variants the early aircraft were designated III (Short Range) and the others III (Long Range).

Eight hundred IIIAs were earmarked for the RAF, these being the first Hudsons to be delivered under Lend Lease. Again, there were many modifications to the delivery programme, and from the batch BW361-767 only 151 reached the RAF. Deliveries to the RAAF, RCAF, RNZAF, the US Navy and 153 to the USAAF accounted for the remainder. Similarly, from FH167-466 very few joined RAF squadrons. FK731-813 made up the remainder of the IIIA production.

Five versions of the Hudson were used by the USAAF. First came the AT-18, 217 of which were ordered in 1942, and used mainly as target tugs. A further 83 AT-18As without dorsal turrets were employed as navigation trainers. Three versions of the A-29 saw USAAF service, the A-29 being

Above: *Hudson T9303 taxiing. This particular aircraft reached Britain in June 1940 and was lost on operations in October of the same year.*

first, 416 of them having been acquired in 1941-42 diverted from UK orders. For this reason many wore British camouflage. The 384 A-29As were all transport aircraft. From the two types of A-29 came two dozen conversions to A-29B photo-reconnaissance aircraft. Additionally, the US Navy took over some IIIAs which became PBO-1s, and wore the standard US Navy camouflage.

Thirty Hudson IVs resolved themselves as AE609-638, aircraft taken over from an RAAF order. These, and the Mk V and VI, had Pratt & Whitney Twin Wasp engines. On the Mk IV the D/F loop appeared beneath a plastic blister. No gun position was fitted beneath the fuselage, whereas this was provided for on the Mk V. The Mk VI had later engines and Hamilton Standard airscrews. It was readily convertible into a cargo or troop transport. Hudson Vs were supplied as long or short range aircraft: AE639-657(LR), AM520-702(SR) and AM703-909(LR). The Mk VIs, all Lend-Lease aircraft, were EW873-972 and FK381-730. Hudson production ended in June 1943.

About 80 Hudsons had reached Britain by September 1939. One squadron, No 224 at Leuchars, was operational with them. A second, No 233 also at Leuchars, was equipped with them, and became operational a few weeks later. During August 1939 No 220 took on charge its first Hudsons. On October 8 1939 Hudsons U-N7241 and Q-N7215 of 224 Squadron made contact with the enemy and claimed the destruction of a Do 18 flying-boat, the first enemy aircraft to fall to Coastal Command. During January 1940 14 Hudsons were fitted with primitive ASV radar and, on February 13, a Hudson of 220 Squadron made the Command's first attack on an enemy surface ship—in this case a destroyer. A spectacular operation involving Hudsons came on the morning of February 16 1940, when K, M and V of 220 Squadron took off from Thornaby to search for the prison ship *Altmark*. NR:K located her at 12.55 and the Royal Navy intercepted her soon after.

Hudsons were very active over the region during the campaign in Norway. Then came more patrols over the beaches, particularly by Nos 206 and 220 Squadrons, during the evacuation from Dunkirk. After the fall of France, Hudsons were based in Iceland for operations over Northern waters and the Atlantic. An exciting event of the period was the capture of the U-boat U570 by UA:S. Off the east and southern shores of Britain, Hudsons engaged in an increasingly costly battle by day and night against enemy shipping until the latter, heavily defended, made the attacks too expensive and the Hudsons were withdrawn. On May 28 1943 a Hudson of 608 Squadron became the first RAF aircraft to sink a U-boat with rocket projectiles.

The Hudson element of Coastal Command reached peak strength in 1942. By mid-1941 six squadrons, Nos 206, 220, 224, 233, 269 and 320, were operating. Six months later there were nine, since 53, 407 and 608 had been added. Two more, 48 and 59, were equipping. By mid-1942 the strength stood at ten operational squadrons but, during the succeeding months, it rapidly fell to six, of which only two were British-based. Crews for the squadrons were trained at No 1(C)OTU at Silloth where P5143, subject of the Airfix model, spent many months, following about a year's duty with 206 Squadron.

No 279 Squadron was formed at Bircham Newton in November 1941 as an air-sea rescue unit, equipped with Hudsons. In 1942 development work was hastened of a lifeboat to be carried in the belly of the Hudson, and dropped to the crew of ditched aircraft. Its operational debut was made on May 5 1943 by W of 279 Squadron, when a lifeboat was dropped to the crew of a Halifax of 102 Squadron. The next drop was on July 14, to the crew of a Wellington of 12 OTU. Hudsons used by the squadron were of various marks, and included T9406:L, V8998:J, EW922:Z and FH356:A. These had the green-grey-white finish, with black letter ahead of the roundel and black serials. The aircraft were frequently detached for service before the squadron moved to Thornaby in November 1944 to receive Warwicks and thereby severing Bircham Newton's long link with the Hudson.

A necessarily brief summary of the squadrons which used Hudsons, and respective examples, follows.

No 48 Squadron received Mk Vs at Limavady in August 1941, including AM801. A few weeks later '48' claimed its first U-boat sinking. During October it moved to Skitten for strikes off Norway, and to Gibraltar in November 1942, from where it returned to re-equip in February 1944. Its aircraft, coded OY, included AM808, EW905:B in use June 1943, and FK:410:Y in use April 1943. No 53 Sqn received Hudsons at Bircham Newton in August 1941, moved to St Eval two months later and to Limavady in December. After moving to North Coates in February and back to St Eval in May, it proceeded to the USA to demonstrate British techniques and upon its return its Hudsons, eg V9096, AM827, were replaced.

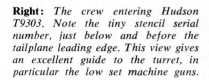

Right: *The crew entering Hudson T9303. Note the tiny stencil serial number, just below and before the tailplane leading edge. This view gives an excellent guide to the turret, in particular the low set machine guns.*

Hudsons were received by 59 Squadron in September 1941, and were used for 'night rovers' from North Coates and Thorney Island, and for convoy escort and anti-submarine duties. Coded TR, its aircraft included AM580, AM666 and FH426 in use July 1942. No 62 Squadron in Malaya received Hudsons at the time of the Japanese invasion, and operated them from Palembang on reconnaissance and bombing attacks prior to with-drawal from Java. No 62 Squadron later operated in a transport role, its

Above: *A Hudson Mk 1, unit unknown, fitted with propellers common to the Mk 2* (J. F. Bradley).

aircraft in March 1943 including AE518:Y and V9124:G.

Nos 117, 163 and 194 Squadrons overseas performed likewise. 117's Hudsons included FK477 and FK481: 163's EW884, FH279 and FK741. No 194 used mainly Mk VIs. Formed at Bircham Newton in May 1941, No 200 Squadron proceeded overseas the following month taking its Hudson IVs like AE626:K and AE622:Y to Bathurst for anti-submarine and convoy patrols. AE575:H and FH282:B had the white/grey-green finish with red individual letters.

Most photographed of all Hudson squadrons, No 206 received them in March-April 1940 and operated from Bircham Newton until August 1941, when it moved to Aldergrove. Prior to this it had detachments at St Eval and AE613:B was among the aircraft used there. On July 8 1941 it crashed in the sea. A Sunderland alighted to pick up the crew but was damaged and could not get away. Eventually the crews of both aircraft were picked up by a destroyer which had to sink the Sunderland by gunfire. Among 206's aircraft were VX-F:P5143, VX-V:P5151, VX-K:T9346 which had the Dark Green/Dark Earth/Sky finish with grey codes. In April 1941 I noted AE620:VX-F and AE615:VX-X with black undersurfaces. The squadron was re-equipped at Benbecula in 1942.

No 220 Squadron was largely equipped in September 1939, its early aircraft including N7230, N7231 and N7237. It moved to Wick during April 1941. AM815:NR-D wore the usual Dark Green/Dark Earth/Sky finish. No 233 Squadron operated from Leuchars on North Sea patrols before moving to Aldergrove for convoy escort work in February 1941. From July 1942 until February 1944 it flew anti-submarine patrols from Gibraltar, its aircraft having included T9277:QX-W, N7251 and T9273.

The first Hudson squadron, 224 which began to equip in May 1939 at Leuchars and initially received N7210-N7222 inclusive, spent periods at Aldergrove. Coded QA its later aircraft included AM827 and AM530.

No 267 Squadron was formed on August 19 1940 from the Communications Flight at Heliopolis, Egypt, and was partially equipped with Hudson transports, including KW-B:EW884 and KW:S-FK507 with red codes. 269 Squadron, which spent a considerable time in Iceland, was formed in October 1939 at Wick. UA:N-T9465 was one of its aircraft.

The Dutch squadron, No 320, formed at Carew Cheriton on January 18 1941 from an earlier Dutch formation. Its Hudson operations commenced on February 22. Late March it moved to Leuchars where the aircraft currently in use included NO-K:T9381 and T9380:NO-H. It moved to Bircham Newton on April 21 1942, and its Hudsons in grey-green finish with black under-sides (which did not extend up the fuselage sides) included AM939:NO-E and V9122:NO-N. Many night operations were flown for which the partly black EW924:NO-D and EW910:NO-L were in use in September 1942. It gave up Hudsons in March 1943.

No 320, operated from Bircham Newton from late 1940, when NO:Y-N7302 was in use. No 353 Squadron, formed in June 1942 at Dum Dum, came under 221 Group and was, at that time, the only GR squadron in India; it operated mainly Mk IIIs. No 357 formed at Chaklala during February 1944 and used IIIs, such as FH333. A particularly successful strike squadron was No 407, based at North Coates in 1941, and later operated from Bircham Newton. It took part in the 'thousand bomber raid' on June 25-26 1942 (during which participants included A:V9092 and M:AM882 of 224 Squadron). Before moving to St Eval for anti-submarine patrols, T9357:RR-F and AM597:RR-F were used by 407. No 500 Squadron received Hudsons in the spring of 1942 at Stornoway, and later moved to North Africa where it received Venturas in 1944; AM660 was used by the squadron. Another Coastal Command squadron which used Hudsons was No 608. It flew its first operation on August 11 1941, a convoy escort, when AM686:D, AM559:H and AM610:L were used. Throughout 1942 it was active using among others AM810:F, V9108:W and AE644:V. At the end of 1942 it was transferred to North Africa. By May 1943 its aircraft included F:AM876 and Z:FK717.

In addition to these, Hudsons found their ways to a multitude of sundry units. Operational training was provided at No 1 OTU where aircraft included P5156 and P5152 and at 6 OTU whose machines included P5158 and P5159. No 24 Communications Squadron had a few (eg, N7275) and the ATA used them for transport purposes. The Photographic Development Unit had some such as P5139. Possibly the most exotic specimens of all were those rare examples which found their way to 161 Squadron for agent dropping, like T9405. These wore the unit's red codes, and had dark grey and dark green upper surfaces. Their black under-sides extended up the sides of the fuselages as on bombers.

Differences between the marks were, from a modeller's point of view, slight. Therefore the Airfix model may easily be finished to any requirement. Additionally, it could be completed as a civil Lockheed 14—and doubtless the adventurous will enjoy incorporating parts of it in a Ventura.

Below: *Nicely 'rigged' shot of the Airfix Hudson model 'in flight'. This is a good example of model photography techniques. A large 'sky' background is used, predominantly cloud to conceal the white cotton used to suspend the model. Segments of transparent plastic card have been cemented in place of the propeller blades to give a realistic 'spinning' effect.*

WHAT?

WHERE?

WHEN?

In the last edition of the Annual our picture quiz proved a highly popular feature. This time we've made it a little more difficult, we think, with one or two items that need some recognition experience of ships, tanks and aircraft. All the subjects are mixed up this time and we've provided the usual key to the answers (together with picture credits) on page 96. Without first sneaking a look at the last page, test your knowledge by writing out the column of picture numbers, then filling in your answers prior to checking.

1: *What vehicle is this, and what is it carrying?*

2: *What ARV is this?*

3: *What is this?*

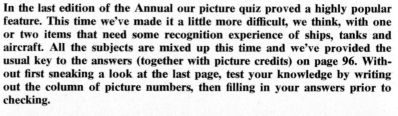

4: *What is this tank and where is it?*

5: *Name the vehicle in the background and the weapon carried by the soldier on the right.*

6: *What is this aircraft?*

7: *Who is this and when was this picture taken?*

8: *This is a French battleship, but which one?*

9: *What was this vehicle originally?*

10: *What is this aircraft?*

11: *Name this aircraft.*

12: *What aircraft has this nose?*

13: *What is this aircraft?*

Quiz

HELICOPTERS OF THE BRITISH SERVICES

By Richard E. Gardner

IN THE POST-WAR YEARS the helicopter has become an indispensable weapon in the armoury of the British forces. Without it there could have been no military solutions to the problems associated with modern guerilla warfare. Conventional 'bush fire' wars have highlighted the advantages of possessing vertical lift capability in conjunction with maritime forces. Limited military action by the British forces in Hong Kong, Kuwait, East Africa, the Middle East, Malaya and Borneo has, in recent years, prevented local hostilities from exploding into all-out war. The most significant factor in all these operations has been the use of helicopters for a multitude of tasks ranging from air-sea rescue to close air-support and air-policing.

Although the total number of helicopters available to the forces has always been much lower than those requested to adequately carry out military commitments, the success of 'chopper operations', especially by the Royal Navy, has been out of all proportion to numbers in service. Throughout the 1950s, during the anti-Communist campaign in Malaya, RAF and Royal Navy helicopters flew round-the-clock missions, air-lifting troops, acting as ambulances, spotting, leaflet-dropping and 'sky-shouting' to terrorist forces. These operations so increased the mobility of the security forces in jungle and swamp areas that they were able to retain effective control of even the most remote districts.

With the increasing submarine strength of the Soviet Bloc countries, it became necessary to develop the helicopter in the anti-submarine role for the Royal Navy. In order to cut costs and delays American-designed machines such as the Sikorsky S-55 Whirlwind and S-58 Wessex were adapted and licence-built in the UK for the Royal Air Force and Royal Navy. The ability of the British aerospace industry to produce good

Above: *A Sioux of the Army's Blue Eagles team. Note dayglo 'Army' on the cabin.* **Right:** *From top to bottom, a Wasp, Whirlwind Mk 7, Wessex HAS 1, Wessex HAS 3 and Sea King.*

Above left: A Westland Whirlwind Mk 10 from RAF Chivenor, Devon. Overall yellow colour scheme. Note crew in rescue positions. Right: A Sud Alouette AH 2 of the Belgian Army, identical to those still in service with the British Army (G. Van Belleghem).

helicopters has never been in doubt, but political indecision over the years has killed many promising designs and reduced the UK's helicopter industry almost to the state of being a sub-contractor. The new Westland Lynx might reverse the trend!

As a model subject, the helicopter is still an exception to the rule. The shortage of helicopter kits, particularly in 1:72 scale, has been quite noticeable. This is regrettable in view of all the colour scheme possibilities and the delicate appearance of a well-constructed helicopter model, but models are available of the Whirlwind, Scout, Wessex and Sea King.

British Army

The function of Army Aviation (the collective term for all aircraft operated by the British Army) is to help ground units and formations carry out their tactical roles more effectively. Unlike some foreign Army Air arms, British Army Aviation is not responsible for the main tactical lift of its troops, which have to rely on the RAF. However, Scout helicopters, and later the Lynx, have a limited troop-lift capability and can be used for commando work carrying up to six fully-equipped men (the Lynx will carry up to one dozen).

Army duties usually involve the following: Observation and reconnaissance in conjunction with ground forces, assisting local fire support and providing anti-tank missiles, forward control of the battle area, and providing limited local logistic support. Theatre Aviation is broken down into an Aviation Regiment per Division. Each Aviation Regiment comprises a small HQ, a Divisional Squadron, and one Squadron per Brigade with the Division. In addition there are individual flights, detached overseas (eg at Berlin and Cyprus) and others frequently visit NATO countries, particularly Norway for Arctic training.

The most widely used Army helicopter is the Bell Sioux AH1. About 50 Sioux were supplied by Augusta in Italy and another 200 were licence-built by Westlands in Britain. This is the standard light helicopter and is flown by pilots from many regiments as well as those from the Army Air Corps. The Sioux can be armed with a hand-operated 7.62 mm machine gun fitted to a swivel mount in place of the starboard cabin door.

The highly successful Army Helicopter Display Team is known as 'The Blue Eagles' and its five Sioux are a familiar sight and sound at air shows during the summer months. For a time the aircraft were painted dark and light blue but more recently they have reverted to the standard Army colour scheme of dark earth and dark green, relieved by 'Blue Eagles' dayglo lettering on the fuel tanks and a large dayglo 'Army' on the cabin front. Other unofficial slogans such as 'Dig Army' and 'Fly Army' have also been observed! In 1972 they reappeared in blue!

About 150 Scouts have long been the standard utility Army helicopter and now increasing numbers of modified armed versions are coming into service. As a result of a general NATO shortage of anti-tank defences, the Army's Scouts are being issued to units in the UK and Germany with provision for carrying four SS-11 air-to-ground missiles. Special sights have been fitted in the port side of the forward cabin and these protrude above the cabin roof. It is possible that more advanced missiles, such as Swingfire, may be carried later, as more Scouts are converted into armed

Royal Navy Helicopters

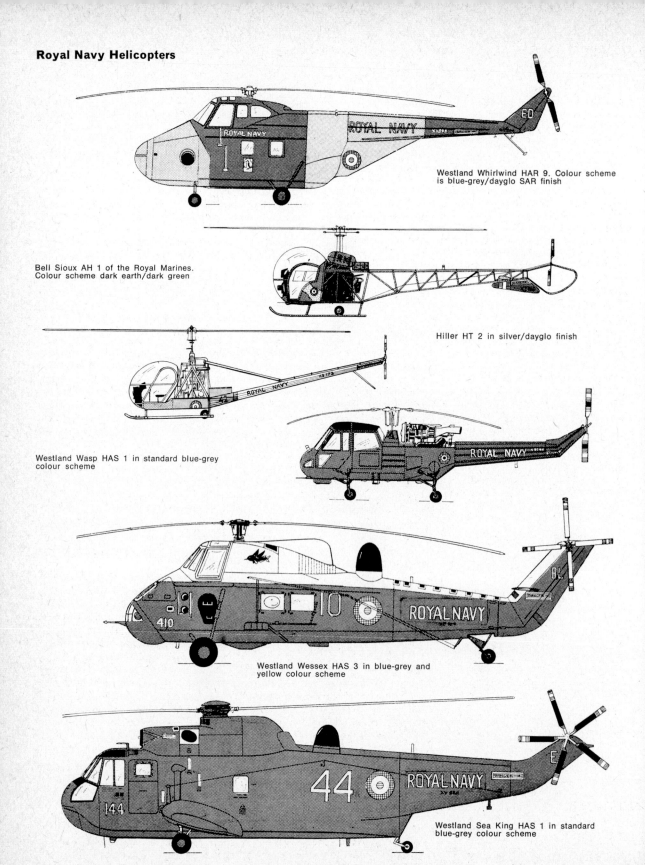

Westland Whirlwind HAR 9. Colour scheme
is blue-grey/dayglo SAR finish

Bell Sioux AH 1 of the Royal Marines.
Colour scheme dark earth/dark green

Hiller HT 2 in silver/dayglo finish

Westland Wasp HAS 1 in standard blue-grey
colour scheme

Westland Wessex HAS 3 in blue-grey and
yellow colour scheme

Westland Sea King HAS 1 in standard
blue-grey colour scheme

Army Aviation Helicopters

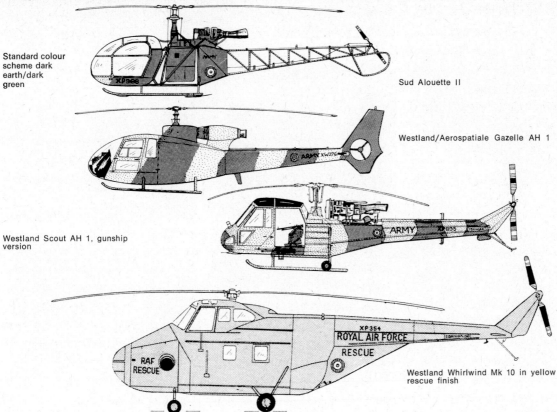

Standard colour scheme dark earth/dark green

Sud Alouette II

Westland/Aerospatiale Gazelle AH 1

Westland Scout AH 1, gunship version

Westland Whirlwind Mk 10 in yellow rescue finish

Royal Air Force Helicopters

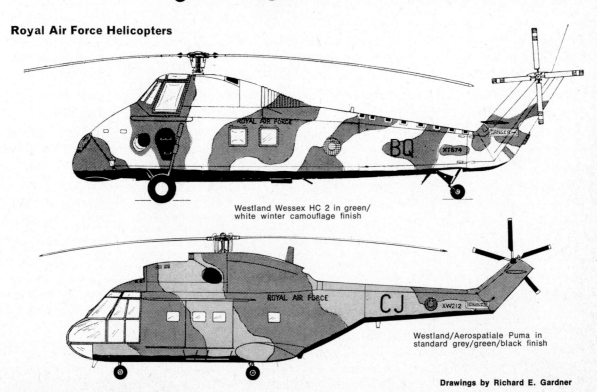

Westland Wessex HC 2 in green/white winter camouflage finish

Westland/Aerospatiale Puma in standard grey/green/black finish

Drawings by Richard E. Gardner

Helicopters of the British Services

Top left: Westland Wasp of the Royal Navy. **Top right:** *Wessex HU 5 number X5490 G/A of 845 NAS seen on exercises in Norway.* **Bottom left:** *Westland Lynx prototype XW835.* **Bottom right:** *Close-up of the mounting arrangement for SS11 missiles on Scout XW613.* **Below:** *Machine gun-fitted Sioux XT197. In the foreground is a typical external load which is usually underslung.*

tank-hunters and are replaced in the utility role by the Lynx and Gazelle. A further modification, operational during the Radfan campaign in Southern Arabia and revived in Northern Ireland for anti-terrorist duties, is the provision of fixed twin 7.62 mm machine guns, fired by the pilot, and one or two swivelling 7.62 mm guns fitted into the rear cabin. Needless to say, rear doors are removed for gunship operations and reloading the fixed guns involves acrobatic antics by the rear gunner who dangles in the slipstream!

Bulged rear doors are fitted to ambulance Scouts to enable one or two patients to be carried transversely in the rear cabin and panniers can also be fitted over the skid framework to carry patients externally.

A small number of Sud Alouette AH 2s remain in service with the Theatre Squadron in the UK as five-seater communications and VIP aircraft. They are finished in the standard colours with black serials and C-type roundels.

The newest 'chopper' to join the Army is the Westland Gazelle. This is a very versatile high-speed machine, based on the Alouette design, and will replace the Sioux in the liaison and reconnaissance roles. It will also have the same anti-tank and gun-ship capability, as well as passenger capacity, of the larger Scout, which it will supplement. About 600 Gazelles will be built for the Army.

The Westland Lynx is not yet in service but already it can be seen to offer much more flexibility than any previous British Army helicopter, and is large enough to lift a reasonable number of troops if necessary. Its high speed should also make it particularly attractive as an armed helicopter.

Royal Air Force

The Royal Air Force uses helicopters in three basic roles. They are: rotary-wing training, air-sea rescue and tactical support for the Army.

In the training role Bell Sioux HT 2s are flown by the Central Flying

Above: *Wessex HAR 1 search and rescue helicopters of Ship Flight, HMS Eagle.*

Above: *The Tiger emblem of 230 Squadron applied to a Puma.* **Below:** *Two Pumas of the same squadron.* **Below right:** *Sea King number XV654 demonstrates the method of lifting an injured crewman from the deck of a ship. The emblem on the nose is a flying stork.*

School at Ternhill alongside Whirlwind HAR 10s. The long standard training colours of silver and dayglo have been replaced on the Whirlwinds more recently by the more colourful light grey, red and white scheme.

The Westland Whirlwind has been the RAF's search and rescue helicopter since the mid-1950s when it started to supplement the Bristol Sycamore in this role. Painted a bright yellow overall, the SAR Whirlwinds are a familiar sight all around the British coast and were recently to be found as far afield as Singapore! In the Persian Gulf, yellow painted Wessex HC 2s (eg XT 604) replaced the Whirlwind and supplemented visiting Royal Navy helicopters on SAR duties. The limited range of the Whirlwind and the dwindling number of RAF coastal bases in the UK has resulted in the Royal Navy having to carry out long-range Sea King rescue operations on behalf of the RAF!

In the tactical troop-lift and logistic support role the RAF operates three Squadrons of Wessex HC 2s, Nos 18, 78 and 72, and two Squadrons of Puma HC 1s, Nos 33 and 230, in addition to squadrons of each type in the Operational Conversion Units. One Wessex Squadron (currently No 18) is based in Germany and the others are based at Odiham in Hampshire, and are frequently despatched to other NATO countries for exercises (normally Norway). Some serve with the security forces in Ulster. An additional Wessex role is that of supplying the V/STOL Harrier squadrons of RAF Germany, when operating from dispersed sites. When in Norway on NATO Northern Flank exercises, the Wessex helicopters have the grey of their camouflage colours overpainted with white distemper paint. This helps them considerably to blend in with their snow-covered surroundings. Wessex HC 2s now serve in the Far East, replacing Whirlwinds.

The Puma has replaced the Whirlwind MK 10 as a troop transport and the 40 examples in service now supplement the Wessex although there remains a desperate shortage of RAF tactical helicopters in Germany.

Small quantities of two further Anglo-French helicopters, the Gazelle and the Lynx, will shortly enter service with RAF Training Command, replacing the Sioux HT 2 and the training versions of the Whirlwind MK 10, respectively.

Royal Navy

The largest British service operator of helicopters is the Fleet Air Arm of the Royal Navy. This service, together with its partner the Royal Marines, flies hundreds of helicopters from many land bases and from practically every Royal Navy vessel from survey ship upwards in size.

Culdrose Royal Naval Air Station is the headquarters for naval helicopter training in the UK. Twenty Hiller HT 2s serve as basic rotary-wing trainers with 705 Squadron and they are supplemented by Whirlwind HAR 7s and 9s. The latter also operate in the Search and Rescue role and are painted blue-grey and dayglo. No 706 Squadron trains pilots for the anti-submarine role and flies a large number of Wasp, Wessex HAS 1,

Above: *Wessex HAR 1 training and search and rescue helicopter number XS884 carrying the 'Ace of Clubs' emblem of 771 Squadron, RNAS Portland.*

Above: *Wessex HU 5 on exercises with the 3rd Commando Brigade.*

Right: *Westland Scout AH 1 number XV126 of the Army Aviation Centre, Middle Wallop, fitted with 7.62 mm machine guns and rescue hoist.*

Wessex HAS 3 and Sea King HAS 1 turbine-powered helicopters. No 707 Naval Air Squadron trains the Commando Carrier Squadrons and provides detachments of aircraft on occasions. Other squadrons equipped with Wessex HU 5s include Nos 845, 846, 847 and 848 Squadrons.

The Wessex has been used by the Navy for over ten years and remains in service in four versions—the HAS Mk 1 for anti-submarine duties based on 'County' class ships and for anti-submarine training, the HAR Mk 1 for Carrier search and rescue operations and general shore-based utility operations, the HAS Mk 3 for anti-submarine operations, including training, and the HU Mk 5 for Commando support in the troop lift, logistic support and gunship roles.

Replacing the Wessex as the standard anti-submarine hunter-killer helicopter is the Westland Sea King. This large all-weather machine has nearly double the range of previous helicopters and has demonstrated its ability to fly 700 miles non-stop. It is the most advanced machine of its type anywhere in the world. Although the Royal Navy is using the Sea King in the hunter-killer role, armed with four homing torpedoes, a new tactic is to employ the Sea King as the long-range search and direction vehicle, and use the Wasp to carry out the torpedo strike.

The Sea King's boat hull enables it to land on water in an emergency, but the heavy-duty winch fitted as standard renders this unnecessary for normal research operations. It is possible that the Sea King will be used as a limited airborne early-warning radar helicopter when the last of the aircraft carriers is phased out in favour of mini-carriers, and other helicopter-equipped ships of the Fleet. In addition, most new Fleet Replenishment ships have large helicopter platforms and Sea Kings can be despatched to these vessels to provide convoys with anti-submarine cover even if specialised warships are not immediately available.

The Wasp is used not only for frigate-based all-weather anti-submarine strike operations but also as a Commando Carrier and survey ship-based utility machine. On the survey ships, the Wasp is used for reconnaissance, supply and transport, and photographic operations, as well as search and rescue.

Most frigate-based Wasps of 829 Squadron are fitted with Nord AS 11 or AS 12 air-surface missiles, which can be used against fast patrol boats or shore targets.

The Royal Marines use both the Bell Sioux AH 1 and the Westland Scout AH 1 for directing gunfire, calling down air support, casualty evacuation, moving stores, liaison visits and as airborne command posts. Flights are attached to Commando Carriers, Assault Ships and other vessels for duties in support of Commando operations. They serve alongside Army Squadrons in Ulster and Norway (where 45 Commando has NATO obligations).

Summing up, the helicopter in its many forms will continue to play a major role with the British forces for the foreseeable future and will probably outnumber fixed-wing aircraft before the end of the decade.

A TRUCK AND TRAILERS FOR MODEL LAYOUTS

By Michael Andress

Model motor vehicles add life to any sort of scenic layout, whether it depicts an airfield, a battlefield or a railway freight yard. In another feature in this Annual Gerald Scarborough gives some expert tips for making highly detailed miniature trucks from plastic card and Airfix parts. If you lack the skill to tackle his sort of model immediately, the much simpler models described here, direct conversions from kits, will give you good practice and an idea of what basic kit conversion work has to offer in the way of miniatures with an original 'look' about them. Michael Andress has chosen these more or less at random for demonstration purposes but the basic Airfix model vehicle kits all lend themselves to simple conversions of this type.

THE POPULAR Airfix RAF Emergency Set provides two nicely detailed vehicles and opens up a whole range of civilian conversion possibilities for your model railway layout. They are particularly suitable even for a 'modern image' layout because they provide a little variety from the usual range of modern vehicles, and one often sees old and rather battered lorries around industrial sidings, coal yards, scrapyards and docks. I always feel that these lorries have more character (and thus make better modelling subjects) than many of the sleek and streamlined new vehicles. Non-railway

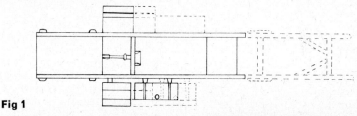

Fig 1

Top right: *1:72 scale plans for the truck chassis. Cut away the parts shown by the dotted lines and move the petrol tank forward to the position shown.*
Right: *The completed truck.*

Above: *The two completed model trailers.*

modellers will find these attractive little models for any sort of scenic set-up where roads or industry are modelled.

My first conversion from this kit is based on the rather nondescript trucks often seen, with a tank mounted on a flat deck, which are used to deliver fuel oil, paraffin, etc. I have used only parts from the crash tender and not even all of these; thus there are some useful surplus parts to be kept for future use. Actually this kit has so many useful and well detailed parts that it would be well worth its price just to empty it into your spare parts box!

If you want to build this model, the first step is to cut down the chassis (part 3) as shown in Fig 1. The petrol tank is re-attached to the chassis as shown by the solid lines in the same diagram. The front springs (parts 4 and 5) and the front axle (part 6) are then fitted as in the kit instructions. The exhaust pipe (part 22) is shortened by removing a segment from immediately in front of the silencer so that the length in front of the silencer measures 8 mm. This is then attached to the chassis. The rear springs can now be fixed in place. These are the top halves only of the kit rear springs (parts 1 and 2), and are fitted to the outer sides of the main chassis girders. Before the cement dries add the rear axle (part 8) and slip the front and rear wheels on to the ends of their axles. The rear axle should be 9 mm in front of the rear of the chassis. Before the cement sets make sure that the chassis rests squarely on the four wheels and that there is no tilting up at the front or back. When you have adjusted these parts correctly set the chassis aside until the cement has set firmly. The drive shaft (part 9) can now be fitted after it has been shortened to fit.

The cab unit is now assembled. Don't forget to paint the inside of the cab parts before assembly. If you wish to add window 'glass' of transparent plastic do this also at this stage. It is particularly effective if you leave the cab door windows partly open by not covering the windows in right to the top. The opening in the cab roof (part 33) must be filled in. Trim off the projecting rim using a sharp modelling knife and finishing off with a fine file and sandpaper. Cement a piece of thin plastic card to the inner side of the cab roof so as to cover the hole. Cement some small pieces of scrap plastic card into the opening from above to fill it up a little and then finish the filling in with body putty. Apply a slight excess of this, then when it has dried thoroughly file and sand it down to leave a smooth surface. Assemble the cab parts and front mudguards (part 23) as in the kit instructions, with or without the driver (part 27) as you wish (if you do use the driver it would be best to trim off his airforce hat with a modelling knife; the jacket can always be passed off as war surplus!). You will probably find that there is a slight 'step' where the two halves of the cab (parts 28 and 29) meet and this will need smoothing out with a file and sandpaper.

The deck is a rectangle of 15 thou thick plastic card 26 mm wide and 30 mm long; fit sides and front 4 mm high of the same material to the top of this deck. Next make three cross bearers of 15 thou thick plastic card; these will fit 1 mm behind the front of the deck, 5 mm in from the rear edge, and about halfway between these two, on the under-surface of the deck, to support it on the main chassis girders. You will have to make them by trial and error so that the deck will be the right height above the ground and will be level. The deck can then be cemented into place; make sure that it clears the back wheels. The rear mudguards are cut from 10 thou plastic card.

The tank is the kit tank, assembled from parts 35, 36, 37 and 38. The supports must be cut down by removing 4 mm from the bottom using a razor saw. The hole in part 36 intended for part 61 should be filled in with body putty. Make a hole in the lower part of part 37 to take part 52 which is fitted with the spout part facing downwards and with the handle sloping to the right. After painting, the tank is fixed to the deck so that the tap (part 52) extends just over the rear edge of the deck. The colour scheme is up to you. I use matt black for the chassis, tyres and tank, and

Humbrol Dark Earth for the bodywork. Headlights are silver. Number plates should now be added to the model.

Another useful couple of models can be made from the Airfix M3 Half-Track kit using the trailer provided to make some ordinary civilian type trailers. In fact, trailers have tended to be rather neglected on the model railway scene. This seems surprising because they come in a vast variety of sizes, shapes and types from tiny two-wheelers to the multi-wheel giants used by the heavy transport firms. A practical point for the railway modeller with limited time to spend on the construction of non-railway items is that trailers add almost as much interest to a scene as lorries and cars but are much quicker, and easier, to build.

The first of these models can't really be called a conversion; it is merely the kit trailer built up as in the kit instructions, except that the canopy is omitted, the top edges of the sides, front and back are smoothed off and a rear light and number plate are added. The result is a useful general-purpose light trailer. There is no reason why you should not have several of these trailers on your layout, loading them differently with boxes, drums, planks, etc. I painted my model a rusty brown colour for the bodywork and black for the chassis.

The second trailer is an easy conversion from the same kit. It's a typical small tank trailer and one of the accompanying photos shows a rather similar full-size trailer. Begin work with part 44. Cut away the deck to leave only the chassis framework. To do this first cut away the parts of the deck between and outside the frame using drill, knife and files as necessary and then finally trim away the remaining parts of the decking which are left on the upper surfaces of the chassis. If you should break the frame

Above: Two tank trailers similar to the one modelled, and **right,** *a more complicated trailer which would also make an interesting model.*

while cutting away the decking don't worry as it can be cemented together carefully afterwards so that the break is not visible in the final model. The springs are cut from the sides (parts 43 and 48) and fixed to the chassis in the appropriate positions. Axle (part 47), wheels (parts 49 and 51), hubs (parts 50 and 52) and trailer bogie (part 53) are added as in the kit instructions. For the tank I used parts left over from the RAF Emergency Set conversions already described but if you prefer a cylindrical tank one can be made from a disposable plastic syringe or rolled from plastic card. If you are using my method cut 3.5 mm from the bottom of each of the supports on the bottom of part 35 of the Crash Tender of the RAF Emergency Set kit. Then cut the centre support away completely leaving only the two end supports. Trim the ends of these to fit between the main chassis girders. The small protruding piece at one end must be cut down so that it is only about .75 mm high.

Now turn your attention to the tank top (part 36). Cut off the projection from the rear edge. Fill in the hole intended for part 61 using plastic filler, and when dry smooth off with file and sandpaper. With a sharp knife trim off the raised fitting at what would be the right-hand end of the top and also the small ridge for the ladder and again finish with file and sandpaper. Leave the small round raised area at the left-hand end intact. The tank top and bottom can now be assembled together with the ends (parts 37 and 38) and, after painting, fitted to the chassis. Final touches are a rear-light made from scrap plastic and a number plate which is easily made from Letraset or Blick figures on a rectangle of plastic card.

THE FIRST WORLD WAR IN MINIATURE

By Roy Dilley

Below top and bottom: *Machine-gun crew in a sandbagged redoubt at the beginning of the Great War. All five figures are converted Britain's hollow cast pieces with extra detailing such as rank badges, buckle detail and so forth. The machine-gun itself is the original Britain's gun considerably modified with the ammunition box lowered, empty canvas belt added to the left of the gun, and a long rear sight fitted from fine gauge fuse wire for use when the gun is in its high angle indirect fire role. The figures are all dressed in the 1914 service dress of khaki serge, puttees, flat cap and polished buttons and badges.*

THE CHOICE of period on which to base one's collection is, of course, very much a matter of a modeller's individual taste and can be affected by many factors, such as the variety of uniforms worn at a particular time, types of artillery and other equipment used, and so on. Unless the modeller has the ability and inclination to build everything from scratch, the question of what models are readily available and suitable for adaptation and/or conversion will also be of considerable importance, but the overriding consideration will always be the degree of real interest and feeling for a historical period that the collector experiences. Collecting, as we know, is more than just the accumulation of models, and most enthusiasts acquire, in addition to the artistic and technical skills associated with the hobby, a desire to become more and more knowledgeable about the background and environment in which the men and equipment which they model existed in real life. To this end they build up an ancillary collection of reference data, books, prints, postcards and the like, all of which can assist in the re-creation in miniature of a particular epoch, not only by indicating the actual appearance of people and objects, but also by conveying in some measure the atmosphere of the time.

World War 1, or the Great War as it is usually known, ended more than half a century ago, but is especially interesting to military modellers in that both the traditional and the modern aspects of warfare were prominent at some time or another during its four-year span. The war opened in Europe with sweeping campaigns of movement, with the immense numbers of troops involved, many clad in colourful uniforms, manoeuvring and jockeying for advantage, with the occasional set piece battle or seige thrown in for good measure. Then the static conditions of trench warfare set in, with artillery and machine-guns dominating the battlefields, causing all attempts to break out of the stalemate to end inconclusively. In the closing stages the war became very mobile again,

Above and right: *More conversions from Britain's lead figures showing part of an infantry attack in 1914 and for comparison one with a tank in 1917. Considerable modification of the original figures was needed to achieve these lifelike poses. The tank is scratch built and the various Germans are solid cast Stadden figures converted.*
Below and right: *These three pictures show what can be achieved using a number of unlikely original figures; those in the top scene are drastically converted Britain's models; the three French officers are the old Britain's AA Scout figure, the same basic figure being used for all three with arm and head positions changed in each case. The figures in the scene on the right are a mixture of Britain's lead models and conversions from the Airfix mechanic and B Type Bus driver.*

with the re-employment of cavalry and the first indications of what could be made possible by the intelligent use of the newly introduced armoured fighting vehicles. Whilst this was going on in Europe, there was fighting in mountains, deserts, jungles and plains in other parts of the world, to say nothing of naval and aerial activity. It was a war of confusion, in which the old and the new in military thought, tactics, and equipment were inextricably mixed, and of bitter attrition in which colossal forces pounded away at one another for years on end without definite advantage being gained by either side. The entire war was reported in copious detail, resulting in a wealth of reliable and readily available data for the modeller to draw upon.

This mixture of the old and the new provides much fascinating material for the modeller, who can depict bright uniforms and sober-hued service dress, tanks and animal-transport, machine-gun nests and cavalry, all quite legitimately in the same period. My own collection includes many items representative of the Great War and, as can be seen from the photographs, they can be employed in scenes and dioramas which are very expressive of the period. Many of the figures of men and animals are conversions from commercial model pieces available some years ago when I began to assemble items of the period. Others are made from currently manufactured pieces, such as those in the Airfix, Historex and Britains ranges, which would provide ample scope for anyone wishing to start such a collection at the present time.

The motor vehicles shown are conversions from plastic kits—most of which can still be obtained quite readily—using plastic sheet and strip to carry out the modifications. This procedure is very similar to the practices carried out in real life, when most military motor vehicles were in fact adaptations of suitable civilian types, fitted with specialised bodywork

The First World War in Miniature

appropriate to their service functions. Horse-transport vehicles are rather more difficult to obtain or convert these days, since even a basic General Service wagon, such as used to be in the Britains catalogue, would cost several pounds to purchase. At such a price, an owner would experience an understandable reluctance to start cutting it about for the purposes of conversion. However, there are still some relatively cheap toy models about, principally in Wild West or farmyard ranges, which can be adapted, with a little imagination, into acceptable horse-transport types and, of course, for the scratch-builder this type of vehicle presents considerably fewer problems than the motorised variety.

The question of a suitable setting for the models then arises. Most of the accompanying photographs are of simple backgrounds, in some cases prints obtainable from the Imperial War Museum, with the foreground work done in wet sand suitably coloured, with trees and buildings kept as basic as possible. Shell-torn trees are effectively represented by small twigs from which all leaves have been stripped, with the end splintered and

The scenes on this page illustrate several different types of transport used during the war. All the vehicles are conversions from readily available kits, some of which have been covered in full in past issues of Airfix Magazine. *The cavalry horses are standard Britain's metal horses with harness detail made from Microstrip and paper; extra detail has also been added in the form of saddle bags and equipment, turned heads, etc, to give an added realism. This sort of detailing can also be carried out on current plastic horses, and is in fact considerably easier to do with the wider range of spare parts available to the modeller of today. All the background detail in these photographs is provided by a mixture of sawdust, sand or shredded peat on a temporary wood base, while the blasted stumps of trees are suitable twigs. For a more permanent display a mixture of Polyfilla and sawdust could be used with model railway scenic materials added to give colouring and texture.*

frayed, and simply stuck into the sand or earth base. Trees in foliage can be bought as ready-made items from model or toyshops, assembled from kits such as Britains range of plastic trees, or home-made from twigs to which are glued small tufts of lichen or coloured foam rubber. Walls, ruined buildings, etc, are made from sheet balsa, covered with brick or stone paper and/or appropriately painted. Backgrounds can be as detailed as the modeller's fancy dictates, but it is a fact that models are often more effective in a simple setting, as was well demonstrated in last year's *Airfix Magazine Annual* by the remarkable realism of John Sandar's models in a plain desert environment.

All the pictures are virtually self-explanatory, and from them, with some creative imagination on your part, and a reliable reference source, you should be able to produce some authentic and atmosphere-laden scenes of your own.

Illustrated here are several more facets of the war. **Above left and right:** *A cavalry colonel and his orderly, a multiple conversion from Britain's figures that could be done quite easily with modern plastic items: A British heliograph signalling party on a small hill. This is quite simply made by building up whatever type of scenic material you are using on a small piece of wood; Belgian Guides conferring with British staff officers, again these are multiple Britain's conversions with the exception of the guides themselves who started out as the driver for the Mercer Raceabout car, a 1:32 scale Revell kit, and a member of an Airfix fire engine crew.* **Left and below:** *The author keeps most of his collection in shallow cabinets which are of the wall hanging type that can either be bought second-hand or, if you have a mind, you can make them yourself; German trench raiders made from Airfix World War 2 polythene figures; two conversions from the Airfix Dennis fire engine crew representing the famous Christmas truce of 1914; casualty clearing station with converted Britain's and Hill figures. In both this picture and the one above the ruined building is provided by the Airfix 'Strongpoint' snap together kit; De Dion Auto-cannon made from spare model automobile parts, the crew is a mixed one from old Britain's figures and the seated men from the B Type bus kit. The figure on the right is modified from the Airfix Spectators set, which is no longer available.*

ROYAL AUXILIARY AIR FORCE, 1925-1957

By Leslie Hunt

The Royal Auxiliary Air Force was once a well-known volunteer arm of the RAF with its own fully equipped squadrons. Today the RAuxAF remains in being only as a number of small control and administrative units and there is a new generation of young air enthusiasts who probably cannot recall the days of the 'weekend flyers'. The RAuxAF was, in fact, a major part of Britain's reserve forces, with a rich history of its own. Leslie Hunt, well-known as a writer on RAF affairs, tells the story of the auxiliary squadrons and illustrates the aircraft they flew. The RAuxAF squadrons were disbanded in a defence economy cut in 1957.

Above: *Post-war Mosquito NF 30 of 502 Squadron; Hawker Hart of 600 Squadron; and Hawker Demon of 607 Squadron.* **Right:** *A Wapiti of 603 Squadron ('Flight').*

THE ARGUMENTS over which was the first Auxiliary Air Force squadron still go on and many forget that No 502 (County of Ulster) formed in May 1925 as a Special Reserve unit, in fact did not transfer to the Auxiliary Air Force until July 1 1937. The honour of being first, therefore, goes to 602 (City of Glasgow), formed September 12 1925; on October 7 DH9A serial H144 was flown from Henlow to Renfrew to become the first aircraft of an Auxiliary squadron. Via the Avro 504K, Wapiti, Hart and Hector the squadron progressed to the Gauntlet and Spitfire and made history on October 16 1939 when, with 603 Squadron, the first enemy raiders of World War 2 were destroyed off the Scottish coast. Distinguished service in the Battle of Britain, followed by the offensives into Europe led by such famous aces as Finucane and Deere, saw 602 ending the war with 'Bomfires', the Mk XIV Spitfire carrying 1,000-pounders. Post-war from Abbotsinch, first with Spitfires then Vampires, the City of Glasgow airmen maintained the high traditions forged by D. F. McIntyre, the Duke of Hamilton and AVM 'Sandy' Johnstone, changing (with the other squadrons) from AAF to RAuxAF on December 16 1947.

No 600 (City of London) Squadron formed at Finsbury Barracks in August 1925, according to squadron records, but the Ministry of Defence say it was October 14 1925 at Northolt and, after using successively the DH9A, Avro 504K, Wapiti, Hart and Demon, the Bristol Blenheim equipped the squadron in 1939 on embodiment into the RAF. On this type Flying Officer Anthony Tollemache gained the George Cross in 1940. The strafing of Dutch airfields in May was followed by day and

Above: *Hurricanes of 601 Squadron* (Imperial War Museum). Above right: *Spitfire of 610 Squadron during the Battle of Britain* (Ministry of Defence).

Below: *Two early Auxiliaries before gaining wings — Pilot Officers the Marquess of Clydesdale and Norman Jones (of Tiger Club fame) with stick: 602 and 601 Squadrons.* Below right: *Hudson of 608 Squadron crash-landed at Sumburgh after combat.*

night fighting over the British Isles with Beaufighters; then came service in North Africa and Italy, where pilots like Wg Cdr 'Paddy' Green and Sqn Ldr (now Air Vice-Marshal) Desmond Hughes excelled. In post-war years operating from Biggin Hill with Spitfires and Meteors the City of London men carried on and, after disbandment, maintained a popular flying group operating a Prentice, Tiger Moth and other types.

The 'Millionaire's Mob', No 601 (County of London) Squadron, also formed at Northolt on October 14 1925, according to official records, progressing through the DH9A, Avro 504N, Wapiti, Hart, Demon, Gauntlet, also on to the Blenheim—sharing with No 25 Sqn the epic raid on Borkum of November 1939. Converting to Hurricanes in time for Dunkirk, the squadron received the Mk IIB version in 1941, only to exchange these for the unsuccessful Airacobra, after which they flew Spitfires from Malta and in the Middle East and Italy, claiming over 300 enemy destroyed by VE Day. Post-war, under Max Aitken, then 'Cocky' Dundas, Spitfires at Hendon were succeeded by Vampires at North Weald until the proud bearers of 'The Flying Sword' had to lay down their arms in 1957.

It was at Turnhouse, also on October 14 1925, that No 603 (City of Edinburgh) formed, in the then-traditional pattern of DH9A, Avro 504K leading to the Westland Wapiti, Hart and Hind. Then came the Gloster Gladiator and the Spitfire, in time for the Battle of Britain when personnel included the late Richard Hillary, author of the classic book *The Last Enemy*. No 603 Sqn bore the brunt of air-fighting which had begun over the Forth in October 1939. Offensives over Europe were followed by service in Malta where the Spitfires were exchanged for Beaufighters and the squadron was engaged on anti-shipping sorties. Finally, in January 1945, came a return to Spitfires for armed reconnaissance sorties from Scotland over Holland. The squadron was also involved in the dive-bombing of the V2 sites. Post-war with Spitfires and Vampires from Turnhouse the squadron was commanded by 'Sheep' Gilroy and other World War 2 pilots until disbandment.

For some inexplicable reason No 605 (County of Warwick) Squadron was formed next, on October 5 1926, at Castle Bromwich, Birmingham, initially with the DH9A, then with the Avro 504K, followed by the Avro Tutor, Wapiti, Hart, Hind, Gladiator and then the Hurricane in which Archie McKellar and Gerry Edge were two of the best known pilots in the Battle of Britain period in 1940. Via Malta the squadron moved on to the Far East where many of its members were taken prisoner after

Singapore and Sumatra were captured. In 1942 the squadron re-formed under Wg Cdr Peter Townsend, first with the Douglas Boston and Havoc, then with the Mosquito, becoming one of the great 'intruder' units. In post-war years, with the Mosquito NF30, and then as the first Auxiliary jet squadron with Vampires (in August 1948), they flew from Honiley, Warwickshire, up to disbandment, remembering with pride men like Alec Ingle, 'Ricky' Wright, Bill Bedford (later the Hawker Siddeley test pilot) and all who had served the squadron so well.

It was not until March 17 1930 that No 604 (County of Middlesex) Squadron formed, at Hendon, the pattern of DH9A, Avro 504K, Wapiti and Demon leading to the Blenheim in which 604 helped pioneer night-fighting over the British Isles before John Cunningham and Jimmy Rawnsley made havoc of the enemy with the Beaufighter. Part of the first night-fighter wing based in Europe after D Day, the squadron, under Wg Cdr Desmond Hughes, finally disbanded at Lille. After the war John Cunningham resumed command for a time and after the Spitfire XVI at

Above: *Vickers Valetta of 622 Squadron (J. D. R. Rawlings); Avro Tutor K3433 arrives for 609 Squadron, Yeadon, 1936; Hinaidi of 503 Squadron, Waddington; and Meteor F8 of 616 Squadron.* **Above right:** *605 Squadron with Hurricane IIs before going to the Far East; and Whitley of 612 Squadron (Imperial War Museum).*

Hendon came a move to North Weald to fly the Vampire and Meteor.

No 607 (County of Durham)—there being no 606 Squadron—was next, forming at Usworth on March 17 1930, initially with one DH60 Gypsy Moth then with the Avro 504N and Wapiti, followed by the Hawker Demon. When war came the squadron, with Gladiators, was ordered to France and converted 'in the field' to the Hurricane, destroying many Luftwaffe aircraft before evacuation. August 15 (known now to have been the RAF's best day during the Battle of Britain) saw 607 defending the North-East of England and at the end of 1940 the squadron was equipped with the first 'Hurribombers'. In India and Burma the squadron flew Hurricanes, then Spitfire VIIIs and post-war it was equipped with Spitfire XVIs and F22s, then with the Vampire. A unique link was that the first CO of 1930, then Sqn Ldr the Hon W. L. Runciman, was with the squadron as Honorary Air Commodore Viscount Runciman of Doxford, OBE, AFC, when disbandment came.

The North Riding Squadron—No 608—formed also on March 17 1930, at Thornaby, with Avro 504N and Wapiti aircraft, transferring to the Demon before receiving the Avro Anson and becoming, from March 1939, a General Reconnaissance unit of Coastal Command. After a spell with the Blackburn Botha came the Blenheim then the Lockheed Hudson V for work in the North Sea and subsequently in the Mediterranean. The squadron was reformed in No 8 (Pathfinder) Group with the Mosquito BXX and one CO was Wg Cdr R. C. Alabaster, destined to make his name years later as a BOAC Comet pilot. In 1946 the squadron reformed with Mosquito NF30 aircraft at Thornaby, later converting to the Spitfire F22, followed by the Vampire F3 and FB5.

The West Riding Squadron—No 609—formed at Yeadon on February 10 1936 with Avro Tutors and Hawker Harts and Hinds. It received Spitfires a week before war broke out. After a magnificent contribution in 1940-41 the squadron — under Wg Cdr 'Roly' Beamont — made the Typhoon a much-feared attack weapon, especially against grounded aircraft and other targets of opportunity. Post-war in 609 Sqn the Mosquito NF30 was succeeded by the Spitfire XVI and then by the Meteor.

No 610 (County of Chester) also formed on February 10 1936, at Hooton Park. Its aircraft included the Avro Tutor, Hawker Hart and Hind, these being followed by the Hurricane. Later came the Spitfire which pilots like Denis Crowley-Milling (now an Air Vice-Marshal) and Johnnie Johnson turned to good account for the squadron. Flt Lt Gaze became a 'Doodlebug' top-scorer and he later destroyed an Me 262 jet. In post-war years the Spitfire XIV was followed by the F22 and then the Meteor F4 and F8.

The West Lancashire Squadron—No 611—was formed also on February 10 1936. It had the Avro Tutor then the Hart and Hind, with one Fairey Battle trainer before acquiring the Spitfire which it operated from the Mk 1 in May 1939 to the IX until February 1945 when the Mustang IV was allotted. After the war came the Spitfire XIV and F22 before the Meteor F4 and F8 took over.

On May 1 1936 four of the five Special Reserve Squadrons were transferred into the then Auxiliary Air Force, the 'senior' of the trio being No 503 (County of Lincoln) which had formed at Waddington in November 1926 and which had operated in succession the Fairey Fawn, Avro 504N, Handley Page Hyderabad, Handley Page Hinaidi, then the Westland Wallace. At the end of 1938, however, the need to expand Bomber Command brought about the disbandment of 503 and the formation of 616 (South Yorkshire) Squadron from a nucleus of the County of Lincoln airmen.

No 504 (County of Nottingham) Squadron had begun life as a Special Reserve on October 14 1928 at Hucknall aerodrome, using Hawker Horsley and Avro 504K machines before converting to the Westland Wallace. The Gloster Gauntlet came with transfer into the AAF, then the Hurricane I throughout 1940, and the IIB, followed by Spitfires II, Vb, VI and IX. Then in 1945 the squadron became the second to equip with the Meteor though the war ended before action could be seen with jets.

Below: *Horsley of 504 Squadron and* **right,** *Spitfire F 22 of 613 Squadron.*

Post-war the squadron had the Mosquito NF30, Spitfire F22 then the Meteor F4 and F8 until disbandment.

No 501 (County of Gloucester) Squadron had first formed as a Special Reserve unit at Filton on June 14 1929, the DH9A and Avro 504N preceding the Westland Wallace, Hart and Hind, with one Fairey Battle paving the way for the Hurricane. In France and during the Battle of Britain, pilots like 'Ginger' Lacey, a top scoring fighter ace, put 501 very much 'on the map' and when the Tempest was received, there were some 'aces' of the flying bomb period, Sqn Ldr J. Berry and Flt Lt Bonham.

Above: *Hectors of 614 Squadron over Cardiff, and* right: *Post-war Meteor of 604 Squadron.*

After the end of hostilities the squadron re-formed at Filton with the Spitfire XVI, then the Vampire F1, FB5 and the Meteor F8 until disbandment.

It was strange that the first number allotted to a Special Reserve unit, No 500 (County of Kent), should be the last to come into existence—on March 16 1931 at Manston—and until transfer into the AAF in May 1936 the Avro 504N, Vickers Virginia, Hawker Hart (T) and Hind were flown. During 1938 the squadron was transferred to No 16 group of Coastal Command and re-equipped with Ansons, doing fine work before and during Dunkirk, at which time Corporal Daphne Pearson, a WAAF Medical Orderly of No 500 (County of Kent Women's Auxiliary Air Force Company) was awarded the George Cross for rescuing the pilot of a squadron Anson which crashed with bombs aboard at Detling. The Blenheim then the Hudson replaced the Anson and Wing Commander Denis Spotswood (now Chief of the Air Staff) led the squadron against targets in the Mediterranean. The Ventura, then the Martin Baltimore, were operated and after the war the Mosquito NF30 until August 1948 when the squadron became the first RAuxAF unit with the Meteor F3. When the squadron disbanded the Meteor F8 was in service; and West Malling was the base.

No 612 (County of Aberdeen) Squadron formed at Dyce aerodrome on June 1 1937 with the Avro Tutor and Hawker Hart (T). Then it had the Hawker Hector before receiving the Anson on entering Coastal Command. The Whitley and then the Wellington were operated on anti-U-boat sorties from Scottish and Northern Ireland bases and in post-war years the Spitfire XIV and LFXVI preceded the Vampire and the Anson CXIX which was used for communications.

Also on June 1 1937 was formed the County of Glamorgan Squadron, No 614, at Llandow as an Army Co-operation unit with some Reserve officers as a nucleus. The Hind Trainer, later replaced by the Hawker Hector, was initial equipment. Then came the famous Westland Lysander, some aircraft being flown to France to act as 'spotters' for the Army prior to the Dunkirk evacuation. The Blenheim was followed by the Halifax and then by the Liberator for bombing targets from Italy as far away as Roumania and Bulgaria. Post-war the Spitfire XVI and F22 was followed by the Vampire F3, FB5 and FB9, adjutant-instructor Peter Latham later commanding 'Treble One' when 111 Squadron became the RAF aerobatic team in the 1960s.

No 615 (County of Surrey)—later known as 'Churchill's Own' when the Prime Minister became Honorary Air Commodore—was formed at Kenley on June 1 1937 with a mixture of Avro Tutors, Hawker Audax and the Hart Trainer. The Hector followed and in turn came the Gauntlet and the Gladiator, the squadron moving to France with 607 in November 1939. When only partially converted to the Hurricane in May 1940 the enemy struck and many aircraft were lost over France and Belgium. One pilot, Flt Lt Hedley Fowler, later escaped from the notorious Colditz prison to earn the MC, only to lose his life testing an early Typhoon. After attacking shipping with the Hurricane II the squadron moved to the Far East to fly the Spitfire and then the Thunderbolt. Post-war from Biggin Hill the Spitfire XIV, F21 and F22 were succeeded by the Meteor F4 and F8 and, for a time, the Walrus now in the Fleet Air Arm Museum was used as a squadron 'hack'. This most unusual RAuxAF type was typical of the resource shown by reserve squadrons when official funds were short; the Walrus was purchased by squadron funds.

It was in May of 1925 that No 502 (Ulster) Squadron formed as the very first Special Reserve unit, flying the Vickers Vimy, Handley Page Hyderabad, Vickers Virginia and Westland Wallace before becoming the last of the Special Reserve units to transfer into the AAF on July 1, 1937. The Hawker Hart and Hind paved the way for the Anson as 502 Squadron entered Coastal Command, doing magnificent work pioneering Air-to-Surface radar with their Whitleys. These were followed by the Halifax and finally by the Mosquito B25. After the war the Mosquito NF30 was first used, later exchanged for the Spitfire F22 and then for the Vampire FB5 and FB9.

It was at Doncaster airport on November 1 1938 that No 616 (South Yorkshire) Squadron formed from a nucleus of the disbanded 503 Squadron. The initial type used, the Hind, gave way to the Gloster Gauntlet and then to the Spitfire I, II, VI and VII. The honour of being the RAF's first jet squadron—with the Meteor I and III from 1944—under ex-602 Sqn Sgt-Pilot (later Wing Commander) Andrew McDowall, was well-deserved. After the war came a short spell with Mosquito NF30, then a return to the Meteor, the F3 and F8 being flown from Finningley.

Last of the AAF units, No 613 (City of Manchester) did not form until February 1 1939 at Ringway, but by May 1940 its Hectors were bombing guns near Calais and its Lysanders were supply-dropping to the trapped British soldiers besieged in this area. The North American Tomahawk was followed by the Mustang in the Army Co-operation role and then came the Mosquito FBVI and epic pinpoint raids like the attack on Gestapo HQ at The Hague, led by Wg Cdr (later AVM) Bob Bateson. Post-war the Spitfire XIV and F22 from Ringway led to the Vampire and training at Woodford, the Avro airfield, before disbandment in March 1957.

To this all-too-brief coverage of the pre-war AAF squadrons must be added a footnote. In December 1950 No 622 Squadron was re-formed at Blackbushe, Surrey, as a RAuxAF squadron for transport duties, using the Vickers Valetta and Nos 661, 662, 663, 664 and 666 Squadrons were formed equipped with the Auster AOP5 (and some with additional Tiger Moth aircraft). These were known as Auxiliary units, with their flights numbered from 1953 to 1968, usually three flights to a squadron based at various satellite airfields. These new units owed their existence to the Korean War emergency when Britain's forces began to be built up again after the post-1945 run-down.

The end of the Royal Auxiliary Air Force came with almost indecent haste in 1957 when the major defence review which followed the Suez affair decided that the end of the manned aircraft was in sight. Massive cuts were made in all the British fighting services and an almost immediate economy was effected by disbanding the reserve fliers. Only a few radar and administrative units now remain to carry the proud title of the Royal Auxiliary Air Force, the enthusiastic 'weekend fliers' who made such a useful contribution to Britain's air power in both war and peace.

Below, *top to bottom: 611 Squadron take-off from Biggin Hill* (Sport & General); *Vampire of 501 Squadron* (Ministry of Defence); *Meteors of 500 Squadron at Ta-Kali, Malta; and Gladiator of 615 Squadron in France, 1940.*

ITALIAN ARMY IN THE DESERT

By George Gush

Above: *Bersaglieri riflemen converted from the Airfix Japanese figures with the use of body putty and a sharp knife.*

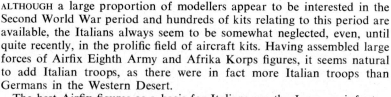

ALTHOUGH a large proportion of modellers appear to be interested in the Second World War period and hundreds of kits relating to this period are available, the Italians always seem to be somewhat neglected, even, until quite recently, in the prolific field of aircraft kits. Having assembled large forces of Airfix Eighth Army and Afrika Korps figures, it seems natural to add Italian troops, as there were in fact more Italian troops than Germans in the Western Desert.

The best Airfix figures as a basis for Italians are the Japanese infantry. Many Italian troops in the desert wore jackets and rather baggy trousers with puttees and for this outfit the Japanese figure needs no alteration. They also wore shirt and shorts and for this Eighth Army or Afrika Korps

Steel helmet | Bersaglieri cap | Side cap

Above: *Italian infantry obscured by smoke and dust in typical baggy pants and sun helmets de-bussing from trucks during the battle of Tobruk. Note the small infantry gun and what is probably a 6.5 mm Breda to the right of the picture.*
Below: *Water supply in the desert, an Italian Airforce water wagon supplies Italian troops with water in buckets. Note the baggy shorts and two types of cap being worn; a sidecap by the Airforce driver and a topee by the soldier on the right who is in charge of the water rationing and is probably a sergeant.*

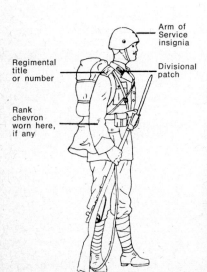

Arm of Service insignia

Regimental title or number

Divisional patch

Rank chevron worn here, if any

Above top: *Italian troops advancing behind an M 13/40 tank in a typical wargames scene.* **Above bottom:** *More conversions from the Japanese figures, this time representing the 6.5 mm Breda and the Austrian 8 mm 07/12 Schwarzlose which can be modelled by altering the machine-gun supplied with the German World War 1 set. The figures making up the crew are from the Afrika Korps and Japanese sets.*

Officer's cap

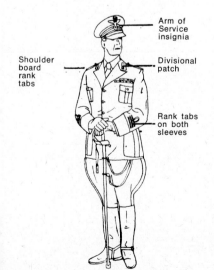

Arm of Service insignia

Shoulder board rank tabs

Divisional patch

Rank tabs on both sleeves

Italian Army in the Desert

ARM OF SERVICE INSIGNIA

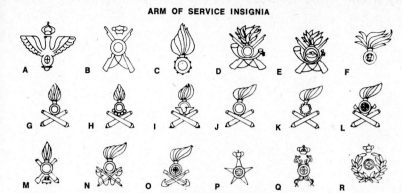

A: General and General staff. **B:** Infantry. **C:** Grenadiers. **D:** Bersaglieri. **E:** Armoured infantry. **F:** Security Police. **G:** Corps artillery. **H:** Field artillery. **I:** Anti-aircraft artillery. **J:** Divisional artillery. **K:** Motorised Divisional artillery. **L:** Armoured Division artillery. **M:** Armoured personnel. **N:** Engineers. **O:** Bridging troops. **P:** Administrative troops. **Q:** Medical officers, including Vets. **R:** Supply troops.

RANK BADGES

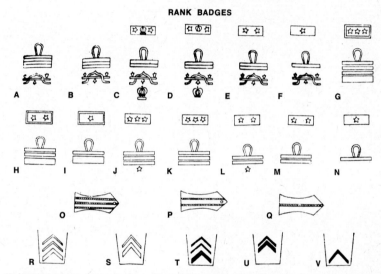

A: Marshal of the Army. **B:** Army General. **C:** Senior Army General. **D:** Corps General. **E:** Divisional General. **F:** Brigadier General. **G:** Colonel. **H:** Lieutenant Colonel. **I:** Major. **J:** Staff Captain. **K:** Captain. **L:** Staff Lieutenant. **M:** 1st Lieutenant. **N:** 2nd Lieutenant. **O:** Sergeant-Major. **P:** Colour Sergeant. **Q:** Staff Sergeant. **R:** Senior Sergeant. **S:** Sergeant. **T:** Corporal. **U:** Lance-Corporal. **V:** Senior Private.

Note: These ranks are approximate as in many cases there is no exact British equivalent and are only given as a guide to the modeller.

figures can be used. The Japanese helmet is very similar in shape to the Italian one and in this small scale requires no modification, while the Japanese peaked cap can easily be carved with a razor blade into an Italian forage-cap (similar to the British cap of 1939-40). For more variety in headgear (and there appears to have been a good deal of variation in the actual dress of Italian units) the Italian sun-helmet, which was of normal topee pattern, can be modelled in Humbrol Body Putty or Plastic Padding. It is best to use an Airfix Cowboy head for this, first glueing or pinning the head to a Japanese body, as the broad-brimmed hat gives better support for the modelling material. For extra colour, Body Putty on a steel helmet or topee can be modelled to represent the dark green cocks' plumes of the Bersaglieri (who wore this ornament into action).

In Europe, Italian uniforms were grey-green, but in North Africa they were khaki, there being at least two distinct shades, one about the same as British khaki drill, the other a good deal darker and rather greener. Photos often show a man wearing a jacket of one shade and trousers of the other. Steel and sun-helmets were a lightish sand colour. Belts were brown leather or canvas, and haversacks were canvas. A British intelli-

Above: *Italian artillerymen operating a German Flak 18 in the desert. Note the tripod-mounted range taker at right and the two different types of headgear worn by the officers in the picture.*

gence manual says black boots, an American one brown, so take your pick. When shorts and socks were worn, the socks were normally rolled down and should be painted black, with white tops. NCOs wore chevrons (see table). These were about 2 inches across and could be worn as shown just above the cuff, or reversed above the elbow. They also had a single yellow stripe on the cap. Officers' rank badges are also shown. These were worn on shoulders, cap and, in shirt sleeves order, on the left breast pocket. Caps carried an arm-of-service badge, which was also stencilled on helmets. In 4 mm scale this can really only be represented by a black dot. Italian units also wore collar-patches, or *mostrine*, in various colours—maroon for Bersaglieri, red and light blue for infantry tanks, black with orange edge for artillery, white with black stripe for Savona Division infantry, maroon with black stripe for Brescia Division infantry.

Support weapons

The main Italian light machine-gun was the 6.5 mm Breda, which closely resembled a Bren, and Eighth Army Bren gunners really need little conversion other than a new Japanese head, though I have cut some off at the waist and used a hot knife to weld on the bottom half of a lying-

Left top: *Model of the 47 mm anti-tank gun made as described in text. The crew is made from the marching, advancing and kneeling riflemen in the Japanese set.* **Left:** *Two views of the 47 mm anti-tank gun showing details of breech and traversing handles.* **Below:** *Drawing of the 47 mm gun to 1:76 scale. By comparison with this and the left and right views of the real thing shown here, a very accurate model can be made from odds and ends and the scrap box.*

Drawing by G. Scarborough

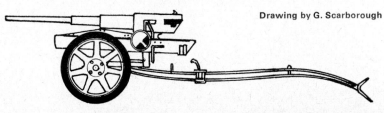

Above: Italian range finder crew for an anti-aircraft battery. Note the leather puttees on their legs and the just visible arm of service insignia on the topees.

Above: Two different types of Italian field guns of 75 mm calibre. These were two standard types of field artillery used by the Italian army in the desert (J. Bramfitt).

Above: Solothurn anti-tank rifle made from wire and plastic sprue, with a crew taken from the Japanese and 8th Army sets.

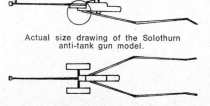

Actual size drawing of the Solothurn anti-tank gun model.

down Japanese figure, in breeches and puttees. Medium machine guns are more of a problem, though the Austrian 8 mm 07/12 Schwarzlose was widely used by the Italians and this water-cooled, belt-fed weapon could be reasonably well represented by the machine gun from the Airfix World War 1 German set, with the tripod slightly shortened. The Schwarzlose had a rather stubbier tripod than the Vickers, a large flash-guard on the muzzle, a pistol-grip for the gunner, and was 37 inches long. The kneeling Japanese figures make an excellent crew for this and for Italian mortars and anti-tank guns.

The Italian 81 mm mortar was very similar to the British 3 inch and an Airfix Paratroop mortar could be used. The Italian one had a squarish baseplate rather wider than it was long. You can equip Italians with various anti-tank weapons. The 20 mm Solothurn anti-tank rifle is shown below. The barrel, which is 13 mm long, is made from a pin, with a 2 mm band of Sellotape wrapped round the rear of it. I made the breech from plastic sprue. It should be 1 mm wide, 2 mm deep and 9 mm long. It could be fired from a bipod, but the wheeled carriage shown makes a more interesting model. Trail is wire and I took the wheels from an Airfix tank kit (return rollers). They should be about 4 mm in diameter.

The Italian 47 mm anti-tank gun, which was supposed to be issued on a scale of eight to each three-battalion infantry regiment and had hitting power somewhat inferior to the British 2-pounder, can be produced from the Airfix 6-pounder. Discard parts 28, 29, 34, 35, 36 and 37. Cut off 15 mm from the muzzle end of the barrel, including muzzle-brake. Cut away the breech-block. Cut away 2 mm from the rear end of the barrel, leaving the recoil cylinder projecting beyond the barrel rear. Cut a shallow horizontal slot across the barrel rear, about 0.5 mm wide. Mount the gun in the normal way on part 26.

Cut off the towing-ring and remove 5 mm, including the spade, from the end of each trail. File down the rear third of each trail to give a tapering section in side view, down to a depth of about 1 mm at the rear. Cut off the part of each trail projecting forward of the circle with the pivot hole in it. The trails now have to be bent, with the aid of heat (a lighted cigarette held close to the point to be bent is one way, but care is needed). In standard form, the trail slopes down from the pivot and has an angle in it further down. It must be altered to run straight back from the pivot and the rear third of it must then be bent down in a gradual curve, as shown opposite. Triangles of plastic card can be added as spades. The trails can now be placed on the pivot in the normal way.

The Italian gun's wheels were of somewhat larger diameter than those of the 6-pounder and were narrower, with solid tyres. Possibly some tank kit wheels could be adapted, but the 6-pounder wheels make a reasonable substitute if filed or turned down on both sides. About 1 mm should be taken off altogether. A paper disc with triangles cut out round its circumference can be used to represent the ten pressed-steel spokes of the original.

The axle unit from the 6-pounder kit can be used, but must be cut down to an overall width of 15 mm. File down the axle ends to fit the wheels. Cut off the part with the pivot hole in it. The wheels can then be glued on; do not use the hub caps from the kit. The axle unit is turned back-to-front and glued to the bottom of the pivot, which should be cut down so that it only just projects below the trails. The pivot should actually go just behind the axle, on the lug intended to take the front shield of the 6-pounder.

Armour presents a problem. My Italians have an M13/40 medium tank, Autoblinda 41 and L3/35 tankettes, but all of these have to be scratch-built with the aid of some Airfix parts and track. Plans for the first two of these (not in 1:76 scale) can be obtained from Model Aeronautical Press Ltd. The Bellona Prints series also now include an M13/40 plan to 1:76 scale, also M11/39. Plans for Semovente 90 and L3/33 tankette are available from Andrew Finch, 14 Doric Avenue, Southborough, Tunbridge Wells, Kent.

Italian Army in the Desert

QUIZ ANSWERS

Answers to What? Where? When? on page 70

1. Austin Champ towing a ½ ton trailer and mounting an American-made M40A1 106 mm recoilless rifle. This particular vehicle belonged to the Support Company of the 1st Battalion, the Parachute Regiment, 16th Airborne Brigade, the picture being taken at Port Said on November 5 or 6, 1956 during the Suez Affair. This vehicle was a glossy sand colour with the serial number 49 in a maroon square above the right front headlight and the Pegasus emblem on the left, again above the headlight and in a maroon square. Further markings can be seen below the foot of the soldier on the right. (*M. K. Brown.*)

2. This is the American developed tank recovery vehicle, the M32B1, on the Sherman chassis. In British service it was called the Sherman ARV Mk 3. This vehicle was attached to 'C' Sqn 4 RTR at Genofa in the Canal Zone, Egypt, in 1952. The regiment was at this time equipped with Centurion Mk 3s. (*P. S. Leaman.*)

3. A preserved example of the rarely seen Covenanter Bridge Layer with 15 ton scissors-type bridge outside an army barracks in Parramatta, NSW, Australia. These vehicles were the only variant of the Covenanter to be used in action, by the Australians in South East Asia. See the Photopage illustration. (*Allen Seymour.*)

4. Medium Mk C Hornet taking part in a parade in London held in honour of Crown Prince Hirohito's visit in 1920. (*J. C. McKenna.*)

5. ZIL-130 belonging to the Egyptian Army and a 3.5 inch folding rocket launcher. This is a patrol of the 1st Battalion the Parachute Regiment some distance into Port Said during the Suez Affair in 1956. All the men have been issued with extra water bottles and this can be clearly seen on the two nearest men. The uniform being worn consists of olive green trousers or greenish grey denims with a jump smock of green and brown and a sand-coloured helmet. (*M. K. Brown.*)

6. An Avro Club Cadet at White Waltham in 1953-54. (*P. G. DeBourcier.*)

7. Crown Prince Hirohito during his first visit to Britain in 1920. He is on a visit to the Royal High School, Edinburgh. (*J. C. McKenna.*)

8. The French battleship *Jean Bart,* 35,000 tons. lying off Limarrol during the assembly of the invasion convoy for Suez. It is a little-known fact that France still had this huge vessel in commission in 1956. (*M. K. Brown.*)

9. Believe it or not but this smart showman's truck is a modified Dorchester Command Vehicle converted to a mobile generator. This is an excellent example of a real life conversion. (*M. J. R. Smith.*)

10. Short S 19 Singapore III flying boat, serial K4585, code 3, of 230 Squadron stationed at Alexandria during the Abyssinian troubles of 1936. It is silver overall, with red or black code 3. (*T. Jones.*)

11. Unusual underside view of a Twin Pioneer taken at RAF Rian in the Persian Gulf in 1963. Note the extensive flapwork which gave the machine its well-known STOL characteristics. (*C. Jackson.*)

12. The much modified Lincoln Aries II fitted with radar and radio equipment for extensive trials. Serial is RE 364. Pictured at Habbanyia, Iraq, in 1947 when the machine was on an extensive and well-publicised world tour. Places the aircraft visited are tabulated on the fuselage side. Badge is that of the RAF Air Navigation School. (*P. Glazier.*)

13. Short Sturgeon TT Mk 2. This is the first production machine of the long-nosed version of the Fleet Air Arm target tug, pictured in natural finish in 1948. The Sturgeon had originally been designed as a torpedo bomber in the late World War 2 period. (*M. D. H. Hamilton.*)